ABSOLUTE BEGINNERS'

# BUSI
# *Japanese*

MICHAEL JENKINS &
TOMOKO TAGUCHI BOYD

*Series editor: Marianne Howarth*

Hodder & Stoughton

A MEMBER OF THE HODDER HEADLINE GROUP

# ACKNOWLEDGEMENTS

The authors would like to thank Richard Boyd for his invaluable support in the preparation of this book.

Thanks are due also to colleagues at the Japan Business Consultancy, Bath College of Higher Education and at the Japanese Language Association for their advice and assistance.

*British Library Cataloguing in Publication Data*

Jenkins, Michael
Absolute Beginners' Business Japanese. –
(Absolute Beginners' Business Language
Series)
I. Title II. Boyd, Tomoko III. Series
495.63421

ISBN 0–340–60193–0

First published 1994
Impression number 10 9 8 7 6 5 4 3 2 1
Year                        1999 1998 1997 1996 1995 1994

Copyright © 1994 Michael Jenkins and Tomoko Boyd

Typeset by Wearset, Boldon, Tyne and Wear.
Printed in Great Britain for Hodder & Stoughton Educational, a division of Hodder Headline Plc, 338 Euston Road, London NW1 3BH by The Bath Press, Avon

# CONTENTS

# Series Editor's Introduction

WHO IS THE *ABSOLUTE BEGINNERS'* SERIES FOR?

The *Absolute Beginners'* series of business language courses has been designed to meet two major, but related, requirements. One is the need many adult learners now have for competence in a foreign language in an occupational setting. The other is the need teachers have for introductory language courses aimed at the true beginner.

The objectives of the series are, therefore, to provide a thorough grounding in the basics of the language, while concentrating on the situations and vocabulary needs of someone working in a foreign business environment. As such, the *Absolute Beginners' Business Language series* will be of value in higher education, particularly in institution-wide language programmes, as well as in further and adult education. Members of the business community will find the series a useful introduction to other courses with a more pronounced business focus; teachers in secondary education may also wish to consider the series as an alternative to general language courses at post-16 level.

WHAT DOES THE SERIES COVER?

Each book in the *Absolute Beginners'* series follows the experiences of a student from the UK taking up a work placement in a foreign company. In the course of the first working day, the student is introduced to new colleagues, and gradually gets to know the office, the department and the working routine of the company. Other situations covered include making appointments, escorting visitors, showing someone round the company, telephoning and sending a fax, ordering supplies, making travel arrangements, visiting the canteen and socialising with colleagues. By the end of the course, students will have a thorough grounding in the basics of the language, in terms of grammar and a range of standard work vocabulary, as well as active practice in using the language in context via exercises designed particularly to develop listening comprehension and speaking skills.

HOW IS THE COURSE STRUCTURED?

Each book in the series consists of six chapters, each based on four short dialogues illustrating a typical working situation and introducing and/or reinforcing a key language point. The exercises following the dialogues provide a range of varied activities which develop receptive skills, including listening comprehension, and establish the basis for active speaking practice in the form of pairwork, role-plays and dialogue chains. Grammar points have been fully integrated into the text; as new grammar is introduced in the dialogues, brief explanations are given, followed by exercises offering further practice of the point concerned. Each chapter finishes with a detailed checklist of the language and communication skills covered. At the back of the book there is a comprehensive glossary with English equivalents.

The *Absolute Beginners'* series provides extensive opportunities for listening to and using the spoken language. All the dialogues and many of the exercises have been recorded on two C60 cassettes, available together with a Support Book containing the cassette transcripts and key to exercises.

RECOMMENDED COURSE LENGTH, ENTRY AND EXIT LEVELS

It is obviously difficult to specify precisely how much time it would take to complete a course in the *Absolute Beginners'* series, as individual classroom circumstances can vary so widely. Taken at a steady pace, the course can be completed in one 15-week semester, assuming a minimum of two hours' class contact per week and regular directed study. For many teaching colleagues, this could be an attractive option, but there would be very little time to incorporate other materials or activities. More conventionally, the course can be completed comfortably within an academic year, again assuming a minimum of two hours' class contact per week and regular directed study. On this basis, teachers would find that they had some time to devote to extending the range of language and situations covered and thus give the course an additional business or general focus.

As the series title indicates, the course is designed for learners with no prior knowledge of the language and it proceeds at their pace. The range of language, situations and grammar is deliberately modest, but this range is covered very thoroughly in order to lay sound foundations for subsequent language learning. The course has not been designed with the needs of any particular examinations syllabus in mind; rather, in writing the coursebooks in the series, authors have been guided by NVQ Level 1 standards for language competence at work, as defined by the Languages Lead Body.

THE *ABSOLUTE BEGINNERS'* SERIES AND THE *HOTEL EUROPA* SERIES

The *Absolute Beginners'* series acknowledges the debt it owes to the *Hotel Europa* series. Though a free-standing course in its own right, *Absolute Beginners'* utilises some of the same characters and settings from *Hotel Europa*; for example, the student is placed in the company which is the customer for the hotel's conference and accommodation facilities in *Hotel Europa*. Similarly, the approach in *Absolute Beginners'* mirrors that in *Hotel Europa* by basing the series on realistic working situations, accessible to teacher and learner alike, whatever their business background. Teachers using *Absolute Beginners'* and looking for a course to help their students to progress will find that *Absolute Beginners'* provides an excellent introduction to *Hotel Europa* and that the transition will be smooth. (Please note however, that at the present time there is no *Hotel Europa* for Japanese.)

ACKNOWLEDGEMENTS

On behalf of all the authors involved with the *Absolute Beginners'* series I should like to acknowledge the invaluable contribution of Tim Gregson-Williams and his team at Hodder & Stoughton to realising the concept for this series, and to thank the many colleagues and course participants – sadly too numerous to mention here – who have provided us with feedback and suggestions. We have very much appreciated their views and thank them all for their assistance.

Marianne Howarth
Department of Modern Languages
The Nottingham Trent University

# PRONUNCIATION GUIDE

The pronunciation of Japanese does not present major problems for native English speakers. The table below contains the basic sounds of the language:

|   | A | I | U | E | O |   |   |
|---|---|---|---|---|---|---|---|
|   | a | i | u | e | o |   |   |
| K | ka | ki | ku | ke | ko | G | ga gi gu ge go |
| S | sa | shi | su | se | so | Z | za ji zu ze zo |
| T | ta | chi | tsu | te | to | D | da ji zu de do |
| N | na | ni | nu | ne | no | B | ba bi bu be bo |
| H | ha | hi | fu | he | ho | P | pa pi pu pe po |
| M | ma | mi | mu | me | mo |   |   |
| Y | ya |   | yu |   | yo |   |   |
| R | ra | ri | ru | re | ro |   |   |
| W | wa |   |   |   | (w)o |   |   |
| N |   |   |   |   |   |   |   |

## The vowels

*Short vowels*

|   |       | Japanese examples | Equivalent English sound |
|---|-------|-------------------|--------------------------|
| a | as in | kaban, Yamaha | *father*, but kept short |
| i | as in | origami, Igirisu | *eat*, but kept short |
| u | as in | sushi, samurai | *hula*, but without pursing lips |
| e | as in | Zen, ikebana | *set* and *net* |
| o | as in | origami, kimono | *Honda, Toyota* |

*Long vowels*

The long vowels are held for twice the length of the short vowels. In *Absolute Beginners'* these sounds are shown as follows:

|  |  | **Japanese examples** | **English word** |
|---|---|---|---|
| ā | as in | konpyūtā | *computer* |
| ii | as in | kōhii | *coffee* |
| ū | as in | jūdō | *judo* |
| ē | as in | kēki | *cake* |
| ō | as in | kamukōdā | *camcorder* |

*Vowel combinations*

Japanese has the following vowel combinations (diphthongs) where each vowel retains its original sound and each vowel sounds distinct:

|  |  | **Japanese examples** | **English word** |
|---|---|---|---|
| ai | as in | samura.i | *samurai* |
| oi | as in | ko.i | *koi carp* |
| ei | as in | ke.i.zai | *economics* |
| ui | as in | u.i.sukii | *whisky* |
| au | as in | sa.u.na | *sauna* |
| oe | as in | ko.e | *voice* |
| ue | as in | u.e | *on, on top of* |
| uo | as in | Haru.o | *Haruo (name)* |

## Consonants

The consonant sounds are:

| | | |
|---|---|---|
| k | as in | cap |
| s | as in | sea |
| t | as in | tap |
| n | as in | no (before a vowel) |
| | | common (at the end of a word) |
| | | dam (before 'p', 'b' or 'm') |
| | | bang (before 'k' or 'g') |
| h | as in | hot heater (before 'i' as in *hitotsu*) |
| m | as in | mat |
| r | as in | roll and loll. 'r' and 'l' sounds are hard to distinguish for a Japanese speaker; the 'r' is rolled, but not to the same extent as in French. |
| g | as in | gap |
| z | as in | zap and sometimes gods |
| d | as in | date |
| b | as in | back |
| p | as in | pack |

Note that Japanese has only one final consonant, 'n' as in the word *futon*.

*Double consonants*

These occur as in words like *poketto* ('pocket') and *kippu* ('ticket'). It is important to distinguish between words of two beats like *ka.ta* ('a person') and *ka.t.ta*, ('bought') which has three beats. Note the following:

| | | |
|---|---|---|
| ka**sett**o | as in | hot **tap** |
| ki**ppu** | as in | top **person** |

*Other vowel and consonant combinations*

Consonants are combined with 'ya', 'yu' and 'yo' as in the following:

| | | | | | | | | |
|---|---|---|---|---|---|---|---|---|
| **kya** | as in | o-kyaku | *guest* | **sh(y)a** | as in | shachō | *president* |
| **kyu** | as in | kyū-ni | *suddenly* | **sh(y)u** | as in | shutchō | *business trip* |
| **kyo** | as in | kyō | *today* | **sh(y)o** | as in | shōshō | *a little* |

*Things to remember*

Note the following:

Japanese has no 'v' sound, so 'Clive' is *Kuraibu*.

There is no 'si' combination, so words like 'seatbelt' and 'single' are pronounced with *shi*: **shiitoberuto** and **shinguru**.

Where English has a final consonant sound, Japanese supplies a consonant and vowel:

| | | |
|---|---|---|
| *knife* | becomes | naifu |
| *Cardiff* | becomes | Kādifu |
| *suit* | becomes | sūtsu |
| *chocolate* | becomes | chokorēto |
| *bag* | becomes | baggu |

Where English has consonant clusters, Japanese adds vowels:

| | | |
|---|---|---|
| *Scotland* | becomes | Sukottorando |
| *biscuit* | becomes | bisuketto |
| *milk* | becomes | miruku |

Now you try! How would you pronounce these *gairaigo* (words from abroad)?

| | | | |
|---|---|---|---|
| omuretsu | aisu kuriimu | sarada | terebi |
| dētā bēsu | pasokon | bideo | chiizu sando |
| gorufu | raitā | takushii | enjinia |

Listen to the cassette to check your answers.

# Nihon Kōgyō e yōkoso
## WELCOME TO JAPAN INDUSTRIAL

> **In this chapter you will learn how to:**
> - greet somebody
> - introduce yourself
> - introduce someone else
> - say where you come from
> - start to talk about countries and nationalities

**KAIWA ICHI** *Ohayō gozaimasu*

**Jikan**      Gozen 9.30
**Basho**      Nihon Kōgyō no uketsuke
**Jinbutsu**      Kenshūsei no Timu Gurosutā to uketsuke no Yamada Keiko

**Time**      9.30 a.m.
**Place**      The reception area of Japan Industrial
**Characters**      Tim Gloucester, a trainee and Keiko Yamada, the receptionist

Study these expressions. Then listen to them on cassette and repeat them in the pauses provided.

| | |
|---|---|
| ohayō gozaimasu | *good morning* |
| desu | *am, is, are* |
| hai, sō desu | *yes, that's right* |
| Igirisu kara | *from Britain* |
| wakarimashita | *I understand* |
| shōshō o-machi kudasai | *please wait a moment* |

Kaiwa ichi o kiite kudasai/*Listen to dialogue 1:*

TIMU:    Ohayō gozaimasu.
YAMADA: Ohayō gozaimasu.
TIMU:    A . . . watashi wa Timu Gurosutā desu.
YAMADA: A, hai. A, Timu Gurosutā san desu ne.
TIMU:    Hai, sō desu. Igirisu kara desu.
YAMADA: Hai, wakarimashita. Shōshō o-machi kudasai ne.

**BUNPŌ GRAMMAR**

## Saying something is, or equals, something else

| | |
|---|---|
| A wa B desu | *A is B (or A is equal to B)* |
| watashi wa Nihonjin desu | *I am Japanese* |

The *wa* here shows that what goes before it is the topic of the sentence – in this case, 'I'.

*Desu* means 'is', 'am', 'are':

| | |
|---|---|
| kare wa Furansujin desu | *he is French* |
| watashitachi wa Igirisujin desu | *we're British* |

**NARAIMASHŌ LET'S LEARN**

## How to say 'from'

Follow the pattern:

| | |
|---|---|
| A wa B **kara** desu | *A is **from** B* |
| Tanaka san wa Tōkyō **kara** desu | *Mr Tanaka is **from** Tokyo* |

**RENSHŪ 1.1**

Listen to the cassette to hear more people introducing themselves to Keiko and saying where they come from. Write what you hear in the appropriate column below.

| [who] | [where] | [who] | [where] |
|---|---|---|---|
| 1 Sandra Peterson | | 4 | |
| 2 | Furansu | 5 | |
| 3 | | | |

**RENSHŪ 1.2**

Keiko Yamada has a number of guests checking in today. Look at the guest list below and take turns with a partner to play the part of the visitor checking in with Keiko.

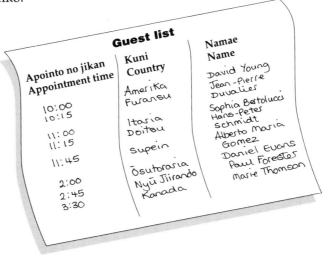

**Guest list**

| Apointo no jikan<br>Appointment time | Kuni<br>Country | Namae<br>Name |
|---|---|---|
| 10:00 | Amerika | David Young |
| 10:15 | Furansu | Jean-Pierre Duvalier |
| 11:00 | Itaria | Sophia Bertolucci |
| 11:15 | Doitsu | Hans-Peter Schmidt |
| 11:45 | Supein | Alberto Maria Gomez |
| 2:00 | Ōsutorasia | Daniel Evans |
| 2:45 | Nyū Jiirando | Paul Forester |
| 3:30 | Kanada | Marie Thomson |

**RENSHŪ 1.3**

Now listen to the cassette and check your answers to *Renshū 1.2*. Repeat the correct answer in the pause provided.

**KAIWA NI**    *Hajimemashite*

| | |
|---|---|
| **Jikan** | Gozen 9.40 |
| **Basho** | Nihon Kōgyō no robii |
| **Jinbutsu** | Timu Gurosutā to Nihon Kōgyō no Ueda Michio |

| | |
|---|---|
| **Time** | 9.40 a.m. |
| **Place** | The lobby of Japan Industrial |
| **Characters** | Tim Gloucester and Michio Ueda of Japan Industrial |

Study these expressions. Then listen to them on cassette and repeat them in the pauses provided.

| | |
|---|---|
| hajimemashite | *how do you do* |
| dōzo yoroshiku onegai shimasu | *pleased to meet you* |
| meishi | *(my) business card* |
| dōzo | *here you are* |
| arigatō gozaimasu | *thank you very much* |

 Kaiwa ni o kiite kudasai/*Listen to dialogue 2:*

UEDA: A. Hajimemashite.
TIMU: Hajimemashite.
UEDA: Nihon Kōgyō no Ueda desu. Dōzo yoroshiku onegai shimasu.
TIMU: Gurosutā desu. Dōzo yoroshiku onegai shimasu.
UEDA: Meishi desu. Dōzo.
TIMU: Arigatō gozaimasu. Ueda-san desu ne.
UEDA: Sō desu. Ueda desu.

上
田

**BUNPŌ GRAMMAR**

## *Saying what organisation you're from*

(watashi wa) Nihon Kōgyō **no** Ueda desu    *I'm Ueda, from Japan Industrial*

*No* is like an 'apostrophe s' (I'm Japan Industrial's Ueda):

(watashi wa) Gurakkusō no Robātsu desu    *I'm Roberts, from Glaxo*

Note that *watashi wa* can be dropped when the meaning is implicit.

**RENSHŪ 2.1**

Mr Ueda keeps a *meishi* (business cards) file featuring all of his business acquaintances. How would Simon Jones, one of Mr Ueda's business colleagues, introduce himself?

**LawrencePLC**

**Simon Jones**
*Sales Manager*

Dodinton · Long Sutton · Avon TA19 0ER
Tel: Bristol (0272) 432109

**Rei/*Example***

UEDA: Hajimemashite.
JONES: Hajimemashite.
UEDA: Nihon Kōgyō no Ueda desu. Dōzo yoroshiku onegai shimasu.
JONES: Rorensu no Jōnzu desu. Dōzo yoroshiku onegai shimasu.

Now work out how these people would have introduced themselves:

1  Thomas Mannheim, Bayer
2  Francis Golden, Hewlett-Packard
3  Teresa Green, Glaxo
4  Gilbert Delacroix, Renault
5  Claudio Morena, Gucci

**NARAIMASHŌ
LET'S LEARN**

Always treat a business card from a Japanese colleague with great respect: study it carefully, placing it on the table in front of you if you are sitting down for talks, and avoid writing on it. The business card is an extension of the company as well as the individual – hence the need for respect.

 **RENSHŪ 2.2**

Check your answers by listening to the cassette, taking care to reproduce the name in the Japanese way during the pauses provided.

**RENSHŪ 2.3**

Japanese people use *kanji* (characters borrowed from Chinese) to write their surnames. These are often derived from symbols of nature, so for example, the surname Yamada is written with two characters:

山 yama
*mountain*　　+　　田 da
*paddy field*

Study the following common *kanji* used in surnames and then work out who's who in the guestlist overleaf.

| | | | | | | | |
|---|---|---|---|---|---|---|---|
| yama | 山 | *mountain* | | mura | 村 | *village* |
| kawa/gawa | 川 | *river* | | moto | 本 | *source/origin* |
| ta/da | 田 | *paddy* | | ue | 上 | *above* |
| ki | 木 | *tree* | **plus** | shita | 下 | *below* |
| hayashi | 林 | *wood* | | kita | 北 | *north* |
| mori | 森 | *forest* | | naka | 中 | *middle* |

| | |
|---|---|
| 1 山本 | 6 森田 |
| 2 木村 | 7 中森 |
| 3 林 | 8 山中 |
| 4 北川 | 9 山下 |
| 5 村田 | 10 上田 |

**KAIWA SAN** *Kochira wa . . .*

| | |
|---|---|
| **Jikan** | Gozen 9.50 |
| **Basho** | Kaigaikikakubu |
| **Jinbutsu** | Timu Gurosutā to Ueda Michio to Morita Maki |

| | |
|---|---|
| **Time** | 9.50 a.m. |
| **Place** | The Overseas Planning Department |
| **Characters** | Tim Gloucester, Michio Ueda and Maki Morita, an OL (office lady) |

Study these expressions. Then listen to them on cassette and repeat them in the pauses provided.

| | |
|---|---|
| ohayō! | *morning!* |
| o-genki desu ka? | *how are you?* |
| genki desu | *I'm fine* |
| kochira wa | *This (person) is . . .* |
| kenshūsei | *trainee* |

 Kaiwa san o kiite kudasai:

UEDA:     Morita-san, ohayō!
MORITA:  Ohayō gozaimasu. O-genki desu ka.
UEDA:     Genki desu. Anō . . . Morita-san, kochira wa Timu Gurosutā-san desu.
MORITA:  Hajimemashite. Morita desu.
TIMU:     Gurosutā desu. Dōzo yoroshiku onegai shimasu.
UEDA:     Gurosutā-san wa Igirisu kara desu. Kenshūsei desu.
MORITA:  A. Igirisu kara no kenshūsei desu ka. Wakarimashita.
             Dōzo yoroshiku onegai shimasu.

**BUNPŌ
GRAMMAR**

## Forming a question

To form a question, add *ka* to the basic sentence:

| | |
|---|---|
| Jon-san wa Amerika-jin desu | *John is an American* |
| Jon-san wa Amerika-jin desu **ka** | *is John an American?* |

**NARAIMASHŌ
LET'S LEARN**

The tag *–san* corresponds to 'Mr', 'Mrs' or 'Ms'. As it indicates respect for another person, it is not possible to refer to yourself as *–san*.

Note that Japanese people put Japanese surnames first, e.g. Tanaka Yuichiro (Tanaka being the surname). With non-Japanese people it is usual to retain the order of the name in its original language, i.e. given name first, surname second, e.g. Peter Jones. Even on a business card for a European business person, the translated name will follow the original order in the person's own language.

**RENSHŪ 3.1**

With a partner, introduce the following people to Mr Ueda of Japan Industrial.

**Rei**   Mr Smith, ICI
YOU:     Ueda-san, kochira wa Aishiiai no Sumisu-san desu.
UEDA:    Hajimemashite. Nihon Kōgyō no Ueda desu. Dōzo yoroshiku
            onegai shimasu.
SMITH:   Hajimemashite. Aishiiai no Sumisu desu. Dōzo yoroshiku
            onegai shimasu.

1  Mr Davies, Plessey
2  Miss Sargeant, Dowty
3  Mr Hall, Virgin Atlantic
4  Ms Philips, Jeyes
5  Mr Johnson, 3M (Surii-emu)

**RENSHŪ 3.2**

Listen to the cassette as some of the following people are introduced. Mark on the list those people who have been introduced and those who have not yet arrived. Tick Y (Yes) or N (No).

|  |  | Y | N |
|---|---|---|---|
| 1 | Mr Furuyama of Toyota | | |
| 2 | Mr Yamazaki of Mitsubishi | | |
| 3 | Mr Suzuki of the Bank of Japan (*Nihon Ginkō*) | | |
| 4 | Mr Terada of JETRO (Japan External Trade Organisation) | | |
| 5 | Mr Kawamoto of Sony | | |
| 6 | Mr Teraoka of Toshiba | | |
| 7 | Ms Kojima of Kodansha International | | |
| 8 | Ms Matsuda of the Kyoto Holiday Inn | | |

Here are some words to describe the jobs people do:

| enjinia | *engineer* | sērusuman | *salesman* | hisho | *secretary* |
|---|---|---|---|---|---|
| sensei | *teacher* | dezainā | *designer* | bengōshi | *lawyer* |
| gakusei | *student* | ō-eru | *OL (office lady)* | anaunsā | *TV announcer* |

---

**RENSHŪ 3.3**

Look at the pictures below of people with different professions. Then make a statement about each person.

- Tim GLOUCESTER
- Igirisu
- Kenshūsei

**Rei**  Timu Gurosutā san wa Igirisu kara no kenshūsei desu.

- John PEARSON
- Ōsutoraria
- Enjinia

- Yves LACOSSE
- Furansu
- Dezainā

- Sue BROWN
- Igirisu
- Sērusu manējā

1  Piason-san wa . . .

2  Rakossu-san wa . . .

3  Buraun-san wa . . .

## KAIWA YON  *Igirisu kara no kenshūsei desu*

**Jikan**      Gozen 10.30
**Basho**     Kaigaikikakubu
**Jinbutsu**  Timu Gurosutā to Morita Maki to Tanaka Yūichiro

**Time**        10.30 a.m.
**Place**       The Overseas Planning Department
**Characters** Tim Gloucester, Maki Morita and Yuichiro Tanaka

Study these expressions. Then listen to them on cassette and repeat them in the pauses provided.

| | |
|---|---|
| donata desu ka | *who is it?* |
| kaigai | *Overseas* |
| kikaku | *Planning* |
| bu | *Department* |
| iie, chigaimasu | *no, that's incorrect* |
| a, sō desu ka | *oh, really* |
| . . . ikaga desu ka | *would you like . . .* |
| hai, onegai shimasu | *yes, please* |

Kaiwa yon o kiite kudasai:

MORITA: Tanaka-san, ohayō gozaimasu.
TANAKA: O. Ohayō. Kochira wa donata desu ka
MORITA: Kochira wa Gurosutā san desu. Igirisu kara no kenshūsei desu.
TANAKA: A, Kurosutā-san desu ka.
MORITA: Iie, chigaimasu. Gurosutā-san desu.
TANAKA: A, sō desu ka. Hajimemashite. Tanaka desu.
MORITA: Gurosutā-san, kochira wa kaigaikikakubu no Tanaka-san desu. Kakarichō desu.
TIMU:   Hajimemashite. Gurosutā desu. Dōzo yoroshiku.
TANAKA: Dōzo yoroshiku. O-cha wa ikaga desu ka.
TIMU:   A. Onegai shimasu. Arigatō gozaimasu.

**NARAIMASHŌ LET'S LEARN**

Here are some important rank titles for people in a Japanese company:

buchō        *department manager (**or** general manager)*
kachō        *section manager (**or** manager)*
kakarichō    *team leader (**or** assistant manager)*

An employee without a rank title is called *hira sha-in* 'ordinary company worker'.

These people belong to various departments within the company:

jinjibu              *personnel department*
keiribu              *accounts department*
sōmubu               *general affairs department*
dezainbu             *design department*
shōhin kaihatsubu    *product development department*

---

**RENSHŪ 4.1**

Rearrange the following sentences so that they make sense.

1  san Gurosutā desu kenshūsei ka wa
2  kara wa san Ueda desu Nihon
3  desu Furansu wa enjinia no watashi

**RENSHŪ 4.2**

Read the following dialogues, work out what is missing and fill in the gaps.
1
OL:     ............ gozaimasu.
Boss:   Ohayō.
OL:     O-cha wa ............ desu ka.
Boss:   ............ shimasu.

**2**

| | |
|---|---|
| MANAGER 1: | Hajimemashite. Nihon Kōgyō ............ Terada |
| | ............. Dōzo ............ ............. |
| MANAGER 2: | Hajimemashite. Nissan Jidōsha ........... Yamamoto |
| | ............ Dōzo ............ ............. |

**3**

| | |
|---|---|
| TIMU GUROSUTĀ: | Kenshūsei ............ |
| OL NO IIDA-SAN: | Amerika ........... desu ka. |
| TIMU GUROSUTĀ: | Chigaimasu. ........... ........... desu. |

**4**

| | |
|---|---|
| OL NO IIDA-SAN: | Gurosutā-san ............ Igirisu ............ no ............ desu. |
| OL NO SASAKI-SAN: | A, sō ............ ka. |

**RENSHŪ 4.3**

Rōrupurē / *Roleplay*

Imagine you are starting a traineeship at a Japanese company in Tokyo. Today you are visiting the Overseas Planning Department. Answer your supervisor with a suitable response and ask some polite questions of your own. Listen to the cassette and give your answer in the pause provided.

**Supervisor**                                                                 *You*

Kaigaikikakubu no Terada desu. Dōzo yoroshiku.

*Give him your name and say that you are pleased to meet him.*

Rondon kara desu ka.

*Say that you are, in fact, from London.*

Watashi no meishi desu.

*Say thank you. Then ask if he is from Tokyo.*

Chigaimasu. Ōsaka kara desu.

*Say, I understand.*

Anō... O-cha wa ikaga desu ka.

*Say, yes please.*

Ja, o-cha.

**NARAIMASHŌ LET'S LEARN**    Here are some of Japan's major cities:

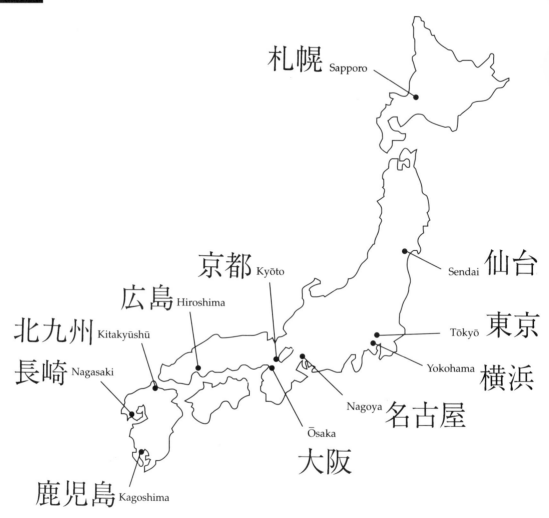

札幌 Sapporo

京都 Kyōto

広島 Hiroshima

北九州 Kitakyūshū

長崎 Nagasaki

Sendai 仙台

東京 Tōkyō

Yokohama 横浜

Nagoya 名古屋

Ōsaka 大阪

鹿児島 Kagoshima

---

**FUKUSHŪ**

## FUKUSHŪ 1

Questions on the dialogues so far. What can you remember?

1  Timu Gurosutā-san wa kenshūsei desu ka.
2  Morita-san wa OL desu ka.
3  Ueda-san wa Nihonjin desu ka.
4  Timu Gurosutā-san wa Amerika kara desu ka.
5  Ueda-san wa kakarichō desu ka.

## FUKUSHŪ 2

Listen to the four conversations on cassette and answer the questions which follow:

**Conversation one**
1  What is Mr Kent's profession?
2  Where does he come from?

**Conversation two**
1  What is Mrs Kawamoto's first name?
2  Where does she work?

**Conversation three**
1  There are two Mr Nakamuras. What are their job titles?
2  What is Mr Kenji Nakamura's title?

**Conversation four**
1  Who sent a fax to Mr Ueda?
2  In what city does the sender of the fax live?
3  From where was the fax sent?

## FUKUSHŪ 3

Practise recognising *kanji* in surnames. Draw a line between the following Japanese surnames and their equivalents in *kanji*.

1  Mr Tanaka        a  川村

2  Mr Morimoto      b  上田

3  Mr Yamashita     c  北川

4  Mr Hayashi       d  田中

5  Mr Kawamura      e  森本

6  Mr Ueda          f  山下

7  Mr Kitagawa      g  林

## FUKUSHŪ 4

**a** Listen to the people on the cassette introducing themselves. Tick the nationalities you hear. One of the nationalities is **not** represented here!

1  Furansu  ☐     2  Nihon  ☐     3  Doitsu  ☐

4  Igirisu  ☐     5  Supein  ☐     6  Ōsutoraria  ☐

7  Amerika  ☐     8  Kanada  ☐     9  Nyū Jiirando  ☐

10  Sukottorando  ☐

**b** Now listen to the tape again and try to make complete sentences about the nationalities of the people who have introduced themselves. The first one is done for you:

1  Jon-san wa Igirisu kara desu. *(John is from Britain.)*

2  Misheru-san (Michelle) . . .

3  Ken-san wa . . .

4  Mai-san wa . . .

5  Maria-san wa . . .

6  Kāru-san (Karl) wa . . .

## FUKUSHŪ 5

How would you say the following in Japanese?

1  Pleased to meet you.

2  Mr Yamada is the General Manager.

3  Keiko Morita is from Kyoto.

4  I am a trainee from France.

5  Please wait for a moment.

6  How do you do?

7  How are you?

8  I'm fine.

9  My business card. Here you are.

10  Thank you very much.

## FUKUSHŪ 6

Rōrupurē

There is a new Japanese trainee at your factory. You bump into him in the canteen at the morning tea-break and start a conversation in Japanese. Make him feel at home.

**You**

**The trainee (Yamada Masao)**

Greet the trainee

Return the greeting

Introduce yourself and say that you're pleased to meet him

Just say how do you do (don't give your name yet)

Ask him if he'd like some tea

Say thank you

Ask if he's from Tokyo

Say no, you're from Nagoya

Ask if he's a trainee

Say yes, and hand over your card

Say thank you and then read his surname written in *kanji*

Say, yes that's right

Try practising this dialogue again with the following trainees:

1  山田　　　Kiichi from Sendai.

2  森田　　　Kenji from Kitakyūshū.

3  山下　　　Yasushi from Hiroshima.

4  北川　　　Tsuyoshi from Matsumoto.

5  川村　　　Tadahisa from Kagoshima.

## SAIGO NI/And finally . . .

Before you move on to the next lesson, make sure that you can:

| | |
|---|---|
| • say 'good morning!' | *ohayō gozaimasu!* |
| • introduce yourself | *Hajimemashite. Ueda desu. Dōzo yoroshiku onegai shimasu.* |
| • introduce someone else | *kochira wa Timu Gurosutā-san desu* |
| • say where you come from | *(watashi wa) Rondon kara desu* |
| • say what country you're from | *Kanada kara desu* |
| • say what company you're from | *Nihon Kōgyō no Ueda desu* |
| • say what your job is | *enjinia desu* |
| • ask what rank or title a person has | *kakarichō desu ka* |
| • read some common surnames in *kanji* | 山 中 |

# Isogashii desu ka

## ARE YOU BUSY?

> **In this lesson you will learn how to:**
> - give information
> - receive information
> - discuss diaries
> - make a schedule
> - ask where someone is

**KAIWA ICHI** *Kore wa watashi no wāpuro desu*

| | |
|---|---|
| **Jikan** | Gogo 2.00 |
| **Basho** | Kaigaikikakubu |
| **Jinbutsu** | Timu Gurosutā to Morita Maki to Ueda buchō |

| | |
|---|---|
| **Time** | 2.00 p.m. |
| **Place** | The Overseas Planning Department |
| **Characters** | Tim Gloucester, Maki Morita and General Manager Ueda |

Study these expressions. Then listen to them on cassette and repeat them in the pauses provided.

| | |
|---|---|
| atsui desu ne | *it's hot, isn't it?* |
| sumimasen | *excuse me* |
| wāpuro | *word processor* |
| dore desu ka | *where is it?* |
| kaban | *briefcase* |
| dare no kaban desu ka | *whose briefcase is it?* |
| kore | *this (one here)* |
| dewa arimasen | *am/is/are not* |

Kaiwa ichi o kiite kudasai:

TIMU:    Atsui desu ne.
UEDA:    Ē, sō desu ne.
TIMU:    Sumimasen. Watashi no wāpuro wa dore desu ka.
UEDA:    Timu-san no wāpuro wa kore desu.
TIMU:    A sō desu ka. Atarashii wāpuro desu ne. A – kore wa dare no kaban desu ka.
UEDA:    Kore wa Morita-san no kaban desu ka.
MORITA:    Iie, watashi no kaban dewa arimasen. Hayashi-san no desu.

**BUNPŌ**

## Saying something isn't something else

Compare the following sentences

| | |
|---|---|
| kore wa watashi no kaban desu | *this is my briefcase* |
| kore wa watashi no kaban dewa arimasen | *this is not my briefcase* |

*Dewa arimasen* is the negative of *desu* and means 'am not', 'is not', 'are not'. *Dewa arimasen* is often abbreviated to *ja arimasen*, making the following possible:

| | |
|---|---|
| iie, watashi no pen ja arimasen | *no, it isn't my pen* |

 **RENSHŪ 1.1**

Japanese people, like people the world over, tend to open conversations by chatting about the weather. Some words you'll hear all the time are:

| | |
|---|---|
| atsui | *hot* |
| samui | *cold* |
| suzushii | *cool* |
| mushiatsui | *humid* |
| atatakai | *warm* |

Listen to the conversations on cassette and complete the sentences below:

1  It's . . .
2  It's . . .
3  It's . . .
4  It's . . .

**NARAIMASHŌ**  *How to say 'this' and 'that'*

*Kore* means 'this one here, next to me'.
*Sore* means 'that one there, near to you'.
*Are* means 'that one over there, away from both of us'.
*Dore* means 'which one?'

**a** Kore wa Pikaso no e desu.    **b** Sore wa Dari no e desu.    **c** Are wa Wāhōru no e desu.

**RENSHŪ 1.2**

As Tim gets used to life in the office, he keeps interrupting Maki Morita with lots of questions. Work out what questions he asks by using the pattern provided, taking turns with a partner to play the part of Tim and Maki.

**Rei**

TIMU:     *Kore* wa *Morita-san* no *wāpuro* desu ka.
MORITA:  Iie, *watashi* no dewa arimasen.
TIMU:     Dare no *wāpuro* desu ka.
MORITA:  *Kaisha* no desu.

1  pen, Fujii-san (*this here*)
2  hon, Kosaka-san (*that over there*)
3  furoppii (*floppy disk*), Ōta-san (*that next to you*)
4  kaban, Mizuno-san (*that over there*)
5  fairu (*file*), Timu-san (*this one*)

**NARAIMASHŌ**    *Leaving words out*

It is possible to leave words out when the subject of the sentences conversation is obvious, or understood by both speakers:

| | |
|---|---|
| kore wa Timu-san no isu desu ka | *is this your chair, Tim?* |
| iie, watashi no dewa arimasen | *no, it isn't* |

---

**RENSHŪ 1.3**

Look over these new adjectives. Then work out how to use them in the sentences below, following the pattern shown:

| | | | |
|---|---|---|---|
| ōkii | *big* | kibishii | *strict* |
| chiisai | *small* | oishii | *tasty, delicious* |
| furui | *old (not used of people!)* | akai | *red* |
| atarashii | *new* | shiroi | *white* |
| warui | *bad* | kuroi | *black* |
| ii | *good* | aoi | *blue* |
| yasui | *cheap* | muzukashii | *difficult* |
| takai | *expensive* | yasashii | *easy* |

1  Kore wa tsukue desu (ōkii) → Kore wa ōkii tsukue desu.
2  Kore wa purintā desu (takai)
3  Kore wa konpyūtā desu (atarashii)
4  Kore wa hon desu (furui)
5  Kore wa fairu desu (yasui)

**RENSHŪ 1.4**

Practise making up questions and answers about ordinary office equipment by following the example below.

**Rei**

TIMU: Kore wa atarashii wāpuro desu ka.
MAKI: Hai, atarashii wāpuro desu.
　　　*or*
　　　Iie, atarashii wāpuro dewa arimasen.

Use the following phrases:

| | | | |
|---|---|---|---|
| 1 | furui konpyūtā | 4 | warui pen |
| 2 | takai kaban | 5 | ii hon |
| 3 | yasui purintā | 6 | oishii hanbāgā |

**RENSHŪ 1.5**

Look at the statements below about various objects around the office of the Overseas Planning Department. Then listen to Tim asking Maki Morita about these objects, marking the statements as true (T) or False (F) as shown.

|   |   | T | F |
|---|---|---|---|
| 1 | Atarashii wāpuro dewa arimasen. |   | ✓ |
| 2 | Takai kaban dewa arimasen. |   |   |
| 3 | Kaisha no pen wa yasui desu. |   |   |
| 4 | Furui tsukue desu. |   |   |
| 5 | Yasui konpyūtā dewa arimasen. |   |   |

## KAIWA NI  *Are wa kaisha no wāpuro desu ka*

**Jikan**     Gogo 3.30 goro
**Basho**     Kaigaikikakubu
**Jinbutsu** Timu Gurosutā to Hayashi kachō

Study these expressions. Then listen to them on cassette and repeat them in the pauses provided.

| doko no | *from where . . . ?* |
|---|---|
| Itaria no kaban | *a briefcase from Italy* |
| nan | *what* |
| hanko | *Chinese seal/chop-mark* |
| omoshiroi | *interesting* |
| takakunai desu | *not expensive* |

Kaiwa ni o kiite kudasai:

HAYASHI: Hajimemashite. Watashi wa Hayashi desu. Dōzo yoroshiku.
TIMU:      Timu Gurosutā desu. Dōzo yoroshiku.
HAYASHI: A, sumimasen. Sore wa watashi no kaban desu.
TIMU:      Ii kaban desu ne. Doko no kaban desu ka.
HAYASHI: Itaria no desu.
TIMU:      Sore wa nan desu ka.
HAYASHI: Kore wa hanko desu.
TIMU:      Hē, omoshiroi desu ne. Takai desu ka.
HAYASHI: Iie, takakunai desu.

### RENSHŪ 2.1

Listen to the cassette tape and look at the pictures below. Which dialogue refers to which picture?

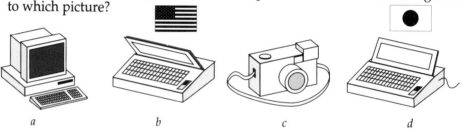

a                     b                     c                     d

### BUNPŌ    *About adjectives*

To make a positive adjective into a negative adjective, follow this rule: take off the *–i* and add *–kunai*.

takai desu                              *it's expensive*
takakunai desu                          *it's not expensive*

### RENSHŪ 2.2

Listen to the people chatting on cassette. What are they talking about? Select the picture which best illustrates the topic of each conversation:

**RENSHŪ 2.3**

In the breaks at the company, Tim has plenty of opportunity to get to know some of his colleagues. Here are some of the questions they asked him. How would you have answered them?

1  Amerika no ōkii kaisha wa doko desu ka.
2  'ET' wa omoshiroi eiga desu ka.
3  Amerika no omoshiroi terebi wa nan desu ka.
4  Itaria no furui machi (*towns*) wa doko desu ka.
5  Takai kuruma wa nan desu ka.

**RENSHŪ 2.4**

Look at the following dialogue to see whether you can put the italic parts in the correct order:

A:   A. Oishii wain desu ne.
B:   *Iie, takakunai desu.*
A:   *Furansu no desu.*
B:   *Takai desu ka.*
A:   *Doko no wain desu ka.*

Now make a similar dialogue using the following words: *ii kuruma, Doitsu no, takai, takakunai.*

**KAIWA SAN**    *Yūmei-na resutoran desu*

**Jikan**     Gozen 11.00
**Basho**     Kaigaikikakubu
**Jinbutsu**  Timu Gurosutā to Hayashi kachō

Study these expressions. Then listen to them on cassette and repeat them in the pauses provided.

| | |
|---|---|
| isogashii | *busy* |
| hima | *free* |
| kangei kai | *welcome party* |
| asa | *morning* |
| ban | *evening* |
| ii desu ka | *is that OK?* |
| ryōri | *cooking, cuisine* |
| chotto takai | *a little expensive* |
| donna | *what kind of?* |
| yūmei-na | *famous* |

**NARAIMASHŌ**  *The days of the week*

| | | |
|---|---|---|
| Sunday | 日 | nichi-yōbi |
| Monday | 月 | getsu-yōbi |
| Tuesday | 火 | ka-yōbi |
| Wednesday | 水 | sui-yōbi |
| Thursday | 木 | moku-yōbi |
| Friday | 金 | kin-yōbi |
| Saturday | 土 | do-yōbi |

Kaiwa san o kiite kudasai:

HAYASHI: Timu-san, kin-yōbi no ban isogashii desu ka.
TIMU:    Sumimasen. Kin-yōbi wa Nihongo no ressun desu.
HAYASHI: Do-yōbi wa?
TIMU:    Do-yōbi wa isogashikunai desu.
HAYASHI: Ja, Timu-san no kangei kai wa do-yōbi no ban desu ne. Ii desu ka.
TIMU:    Hai, dōmo arigatō gozaimasu. Kangei kai wa doko desu ka.
HAYASHI: Resutoran Fuji desu.
TIMU:    Donna resutoran desu ka.
HAYASHI: Chotto takai desu ga, ryōri wa oishii desu. Yūmei-na resutoran desu.

**RENSHŪ 3.1**

The following schedule shows what Tim and Hayashi *kachō* are doing in the evenings during the next week. Make up dialogues between them, following the example given.

| Schedule | Nichi Sunday | Getsu-Monday | Ka-Tuesday | Sui-Wednesday | Moku-Thursday | Kin-Friday | Do-yōbi Saturday |
|---|---|---|---|---|---|---|---|
| **Timu** | | | tenisu | pātii | | Nihongo | |
| **Hayashi** | | | | | karate | Eigo | |

**Rei**

HAYASHI: Ka-yōbi wa isogashii desu ka.
TIMU:    Sumimasen. Ka-yōbi wa tenisu desu.
HAYASHI: Do-yōbi wa?
TIMU:    Do-yōbi wa isogashikunai desu.
HAYASHI: Ja, kangei-kai wa do-yōbi desu ne.

1  Hayashi asks Tim about *hanami* (flower-viewing). He tries Friday and Monday.
2  Tim asks Hayashi about *gorufu* (golf). He tries Thursday and Sunday.

**NARAIMASHŌ**  *Asking 'when?'*

To ask when something is happening, say: *itsu desu ka.*

pātii wa itsu desu ka        *when's the party?*
do-yōbi no ban desu          *Saturday night*

*Itsu* is the word for 'when'

**RENSHŪ 3.2**

Listen to the dialogue between Tim and Hayashi *kachō* on cassette and answer the questions appropriately.

1  What's the conversation regarding?
2  What day of the week will it be?
3  Where will it be?
4  What's on the menu?

| BUNPŌ | *More information on adjectives* |

In addition to the *–i* adjectives learned so far, there is a second group of adjectives called *–na* adjectives – so called because they end in *–na*.

yūmei-na   *famous*                  benri-na   *convenient*
shinsetsu-na   *kind*                taihen-na   *terrible, awful*
genki-na   *healthy, fit, well*     kirei-na   *beautiful (or clean)*

When a *–na* adjective stands alone, drop the *–na*:

taihen desu ne                       *oh, that's awful*
kirei desu ne!                       *wow, that's beautiful!*

When describing another word, use the *–na* to connect the adjective and the noun:

yūmei-**na** resutoran desu          *it's a famous restaurant*
benri–**na** tokoro desu             *it's a convenient place*
shinsetsu–**na** hito desu           *s(he)'s a kind person*

---

### RENSHŪ 3.3

Connect words from the three columns below to make complete sentences.

| | | | | | | |
|---|---|---|---|---|---|---|
| 1 | Kore wa | **a** | yūmei-na | **t** | kaisha desu |
| 2 | Hayashi-san wa | **b** | benri-na | **u** | hito desu |
| 3 | Are wa | **c** | genki-na | **v** | kachō desu |
| 4 | Nihon ryōri wa | **d** | shinsetsu-na | **w** | konpyūtā desu |
| 5 | Timu-san wa | **e** | oishii | **x** | desu |
| 6 | Nihon no hoteru wa | **f** | omoshiroi | **y** | desu ka |
| 7 | Supein no terebi wa | **g** | takai | **z** | desu |

### RENSHŪ 3.4

Complete the crossword opposite. Note the adjectives which appear, and some words which you might not yet know!

**Across**
1  It's not cheap (......... *desu*) (9)
5  Interesting
8  ... *kokujin* (3) (the word for 'foreigner')
9  The number 2
10  Also
11  .... *setsu-na buchō desu* (4)
13  *Kōhii* . ....... (1, 7)
15  A kind of eating place
16  Expensive
19  .... *arimasen* (2)
20  The number 1

**Down**
1  A famous car
2  Is (this) *sashimi*?
3  A meeting
4  Blue
6  .., *ri, ru, re, ro* (2)
7  A delicious orange
12  The Japanese language
14  *Shin.....-na kachō desu* (5)
16  And
17  ?
18  Opposite of *warui* (2)

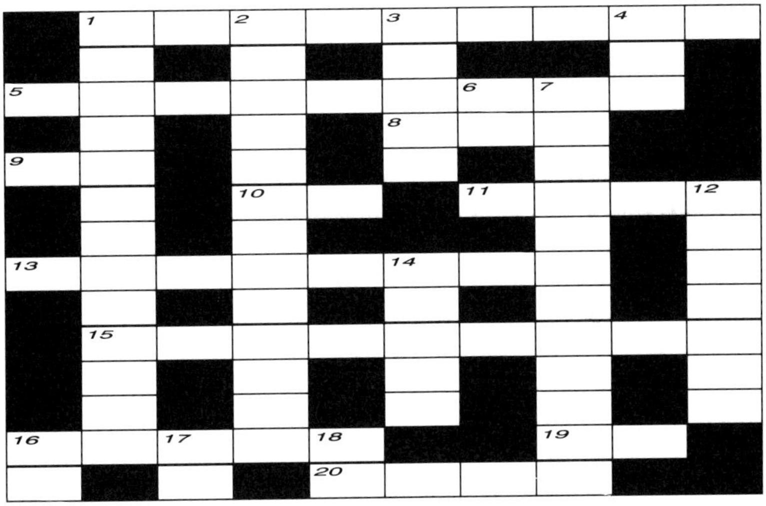

**KAIWA YON** *Raishū no getsu-yōbi kara desu*

**Jikan** Gogo 2.00
**Basho** Kaigaikikakubu
**Jinbutsu** Timu Gurosutā to Ueda buchō

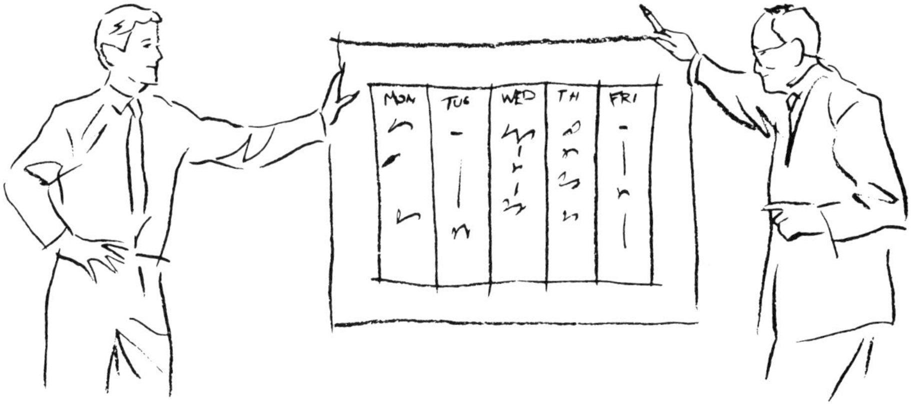


Study these expressions. Then listen to them on cassette and repeat them in the pauses provided.

| | |
|---|---|
| itsu kara | *from when* |
| itsu made | *until when* |
| kaigi-shitsu | *meeting room* |
| robii no yoko | *next to the lobby* |
| wakarimashita | *I understand, I see* |
| raishū | *next week* |
| sa-raishū | *the week after next* |

Kaiwa yon o kiite kudasai:

TIMU: Ano, chotto ii desu ka.
UEDA: Hai, nan desu ka.
TIMU: Kenshūsei no torēningu wa raishū no getsu-yōbi kara desu ne. Asa kara desu ka.
UEDA: Iie, asa kara dewa arimasen. Getsuyōbi no torēningu wa hiru kara desu. Ka-yōbi wa asa kara desu.
TIMU: Torēningu wa itsu made desu ka.
UEDA: Sa-raishū no kin-yōbi made desu.
TIMU: Basho wa doko desu ka.
UEDA: Kaigi-shitsu desu. Robii no yoko desu.
TIMU: Hai, wakarimashita.

## BUNPŌ

## *Saying 'from' and 'to'*

'From' (*kara*) and 'to' (*made*) follow the thing that they qualify:

| | |
|---|---|
| sui-yōbi kara desu | *from Wednesday* |
| kin-yōbi made desu | *to Friday* |

*Kara* and *made* can be used in the same sentence:

| | |
|---|---|
| Tōkyō kara Ōsaka made | *from Tokyo to Osaka* |
| Asa kara hiru made | *from morning until midday* |

To ask 'from when until when', use *itsu kara itsu made*.

| | |
|---|---|
| Nihongo no ressun wa itsu kara itsu made desu ka | *from when until when are your Japanese lessons?* |
| O-shigoto wa . . . getsu-yōbi kara desu ka. | *So . . . your job is from Monday?* |
| Un, sō desu. | *Yup, that's right.* |
| Kin-yōbi made desu ka. | *To Friday?* |
| Iie, moku-yōbi made desu. Pāto-taimā desu. | *No. Thursday. I'm a part-timer.* |

## RENSHŪ 4.1

Look at Tim's training schedule below. Then practise the short dialogue between Tim and Ueda *buchō* which follows, making dialogues of your own by changing the words in italics. Follow the prompts given.

TIMU: *Nihongo no kōsu* wa itsu kara itsu made desu ka.
UEDA: *Raishū no getsu-yōbi* kara *sa-raishū no ka-yōbi* made desu.
TIMU: *Do-yōbi* wa yasumi desu ka.
UEDA: Hai, sō desu. *Getsu-yōbi* wa *hiru* kara desu. *Ka-yōbi* wa *asa* desu.

1   Konpyūtā no kōsu →
2   Māketingu no torēningu →

|  | Nichi | Getsu- | Ka- | Sui- | Moku- | Kin- | Do-yōbi |
|---|---|---|---|---|---|---|---|
| **Raishū** | Yasumi | ◄———— | ——— Nihon-go no kōsu ——— | | | | Yasumi |
|  |  | hiru<br>kara |  |  |  |  |  |
|  |  |  | ◄— konpyūtā no kōsu —► | | |  |  |
|  |  |  | asa<br>kara |  | hiru<br>made |  |  |
| **Saraishū** | Yasumi | ——————— | ►◄— Māketingu no torēningu —► | | | | Yasumi |
|  |  |  | hiru<br>made | hiru<br>kara |  | hiru<br>made |  |

---

**NARAIMASHŌ**

Here are some useful time expressions:

kinō   *yesterday*          kyō   *today*
ashita   *tomorrow*          senshū   *last week*
konshū   *this week*          raishū   *next week*
sengetsu   *last month*          kongetsu   *this month*
raigetsu   *next month*          kyonen   *last year*
kotoshi   *this year*          rainen   *next year*

---

**RENSHŪ 4.2**

Listen to the dialogues on cassette and complete the schedules of the people below.

1   Hayashi *kachō*'s business trip: from . . . to . . .
2   Maki Morita's English course: from . . . to . . .
3   Watanabe-san's marketing course: from . . . to . . .

**NARAIMASHŌ**   *Asking 'where?'*

To ask 'Where', use *doko* as follows:

erebētā wa doko desu ka          *where's the lift?*
Timu-san wa doko desu ka          *where's Tim?*

---

**BUNPŌ**   *Giving the location of people and things*

To say where something or someone is, use the pattern: location + *no* + preposition + *desu*.

| | |
|---|---|
| kaigi-shitsu no **yoko** desu | *next to the meeting room* |
| esukarēta no **mae** desu | *in front of the escalator* |

Here are some important prepositions:

| | |
|---|---|
| kuruma no ushiro | *behind the car* |
| kuruma no shita | *under the car* |
| kuruma no ue | *on (or on top of) the car* |
| kuruma no naka | *inside the car* |
| kuruma no soba | *next to the car* |

   **RENSHŪ 4.3**

**a** Listen to the cassette and try to fill in the missing information in the table below. Tim and Maki Morita are trying to confirm where everyone is at the moment.

| Who | Location of person | Location of place |
|---|---|---|
| 1  Hayashi-kachō | Photocopying room | Next to the little meeting room opposite the big meeting room |
| 2 | President's room | Next to the lift, opposite the main administration office (*jimu-shitsu*) |
| 3  Tanaka-buchō | | |
| 4 | Little meeting room | |

**b** Now, based on what you have just heard, see whether you can deduce which rooms are which on the floor-plan below:

1  ōkii kaigi-shitsu
2  chiisai kaigi-shitsu
3  shachō-shitsu
4  kopii-shitsu
5  jimu-shitsu

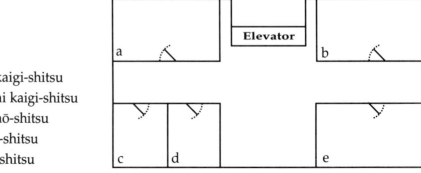

## FUKUSHŪ

### FUKUSHŪ 1

Use an appropriate adjective from below to make complete sentences.

mushiatsui    yasui    shinsetsu-na    takai    suzushii    furui

1  Amerika no kuruma wa ............ desu.
2  Nihon no kuruma wa ............ desu.
3  Hawaii wa ............ desu ne.
4  Nakano-san wa ............ buchō desu.
5  Rōma wa ............ machi desu.

(machi   *town, city*)

### FUKUSHŪ 2

Answer the following questions in Japanese.

1  Ōkii hoteru wa doko desu ka. (*In your country*)
2  Yūmei-na resutoran wa doko desu ka. (*In your country*)
3  Oishii ryōri wa nan desu ka. (*In your country*)
4  Takai kuruma wa nan desu ka. (*In your country*)
5  Kaisha no shachō wa donna hito desu ka. (*In your company*)

### FUKUSHŪ 3

How would you render the following two dialogues in Japanese?

1
A:  Whose book is this?
B:  That's Mr Murata's.
A:  Where is he?
B:  He's in the managing director's room.
A:  Is it a meeting?
B:  Yes. The meeting started this morning.
A:  When will the meeting finish? (*when until*)
B:  At lunch time. (*until lunchtime*)


2
A:  The welcome party is next week – on Friday.
B:  Where will it take place?
A:  At the Sakura Hotel.
B:  What's the hotel like?
A:  It's a big hotel. They serve French food there. (*the cooking is French cooking*)

## FUKUSHŪ 4

Look at the following advert which says which days of the week Aloha Airlines flies between Honolulu and Nagoya. On which days are there no flights?

## FUKUSHŪ 5

Listen to the cassette to find out on which day of the week different events will be held. Note that the events are not necessarily all mentioned.

| | | |
|---|---|---|
| 1 | A meeting. | On ........... |
| 2 | A business trip. | From ........... until ........... |
| 3 | A welcome party. | On ........... |
| 4 | A Japanese language course. | From ........... until ........... |
| 5 | A computer course. | From ........... until ........... |

## FUKUSHŪ 6

Listen to the following conversations and answer the questions in English.

1a  Who is the car owner?
 b  Where does the car come from?
2a  When did Mr Satō set off for his business trip?
 b  When will he come back from his business trip?
3a  Where is the old word-processor?
 b  Where is the new word-processor?
4a  What kind of tape is it?
 b  Is it a famous tape?


## FUKUSHŪ 7

Rōrupurē

It's next morning one summer's day in your office in Osaka. Your colleague Nakamura-san opposite is hot and bothered. He looks like he has a lot on his mind. You set out to find out why . . .

**You**                                                    **Your colleague Nakamura-san**

Say good morning

A-O-hayō gozaimasu

Say it's hot today

Un-mushiatsui desu ne

Ask if he would like some barley tea  (= mugi-cha)

A-arigatō

Ask him if he's busy

Un-isogashii desu ne

Ask when his holidays are
(yasumi wa...)

Konshu no kinyōbi kara desu

Remind him that there's a party this Friday

E! Donna pātii desu ka

Say it's Kondō-san's welcome party

A sō desu ne. Pātii wa doko desu ka

Say, it's at the Holiday Inn

Ryōri wa?

Say it's Japanese food

A-ii desu ne!

# SAIGO NI

Before moving on to the next lesson, make sure you can:

- make some small talk about the weather — *kyō wa atsui desu ne*
- ask 'what kind of' — *donna . . . desu ka*
- ask 'where' — *doko desu ka*
- ask 'when' — *itsu desu ka*
- use the words for 'this', 'that' and 'which one' — *kore, sore, are* and *dore?*
- use adjectives to describe objects and people — *takai kuruma, shinsetsu-na hito*
- say something is not something else — *kore wa watashi no dewa arimasen/ja arimasen*
- remember the days of the week and recognise the characters for them — *getsu-yōbi* 月
- talk about simple periods of time — *asa kara hiru made*

# *Otsukaresama deshita!*

## YOU'VE DONE WELL!

In this lesson you will learn how to:
- say where places and things are
- ask how to get somewhere
- ask for and understand telephone numbers
- ask what time something is going to happen
- give reasons

**KAIWA ICHI** *Denwa bangō wa nan-ban desu ka*

**Jikan**  Gogo 5-ji goro
**Basho**  Kaigaikikakubu
**Jinbutsu** Hayashi-kachō to Timu Gurosutā

Study these expressions. Then listen to them on cassette and repeat them in the pauses provided.

| | |
|---|---|
| ryō | *dormitory* |
| chizu | *map* |
| hiroi | *spacious, wide* |
| nan-ban | *what number* |
| denwa bangō | *telephone number* |
| atarashikute kirei-na | *new and clean* |
| heya no bangō | *room number* |

## NARAIMASHŌ  *Numbers*

 Now listen to and repeat the numbers below:

| | | | | |
|---|---|---|---|---|
| 0 | rei/zero | | | |
| 1 | ichi | 6 | roku | |
| 2 | ni | 7 | nana/shichi | |
| 3 | san | 8 | hachi | |
| 4 | shi/yon | 9 | kyū/ku | |
| 5 | go | 10 | jū | |

When a telephone number is given, the dashes or hyphens between numbers are indicated by the speaker saying *no*.

Watashi no denwa bangō wa zero ni ni go *no* yon yon yon ichi kyū zero (0225-444190) desu.

 Kaiwa ichi o kiite kudasai:

HAYASHI: Kore wa ryō no chizu desu.
TIMU:    Dōmo arigatō gozaimasu.
HAYASHI: Amari hirokunai desu ga, atarashikute kirei-na ryō desu yo.
TIMU:    A sō desu ka. Ryō no denwa bangō wa nan-ban desu ka.
HAYASHI: 637-8812 desu.
TIMU:    637-8812 desu ne. Wakarimashita.

## NARAIMASHŌ  Atarashikute kirei-na apāto desu **yo**.

*Yo* at the end of this sentence has the meaning 'you know' or 'contrary to what you might think', i.e. 'it really is a clean, new apartment you know.'

### RENSHŪ 1.1

Listen to the cassette as a list of 10 room numbers at the dormitory is read out by the *kanrinin* (caretaker). Circle the ones you hear from the possibilities listed below.

| 1 | 121 | 131 | 212 | 6 | 229 | 496 | 387 |
|---|-----|-----|-----|----|-----|-----|-----|
| 2 | 334 | 354 | 323 | 7 | 730 | 217 | 594 |
| 3 | 456 | 502 | 513 | 8 | 483 | 434 | 651 |
| 4 | 724 | 175 | 782 | 9 | 902 | 458 | 311 |
| 5 | 985 | 359 | 401 | 10 | 228 | 469 | 370 |

Practise these numbers with a partner: one of you can be the *kanrinin* while the other listens. Check that you have taken down the numbers correctly.

### RENSHŪ 1.2

Maki Morita has been asked to give the *jinjibu* (Personnel Department) an up-to-date list of the home telephone numbers of people in the Overseas Planning Department. Complete the exchanges by following the pattern provided and referring to Maki's note-pad:

PERSONNEL CLERK: Tanaka san no denwa bangō wa nan-ban desu ka.
MORITA: Hachi kyū san no nana yon ni ichi desu.
PERSONNEL CLERK: Yamada san wa?
MORITA: . . .

Tanaka 893-7421
Yamada 463-2235
Koike 394-5882
Ueda 135-4931
Morita 455-2467

## RENSHŪ 1.3

Listen to the cassette as various people ask for information containing numbers. Choose the correct alternative from the boxes below:

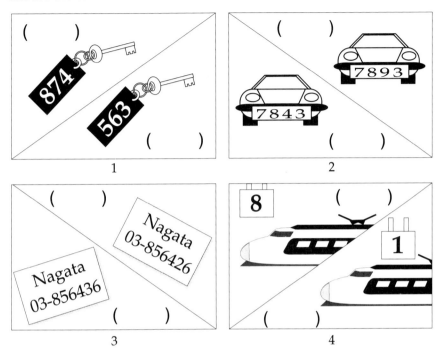

BUNPŌ

## *Connecting adjectives*

To connect adjectives to give more detail about something, follow these patterns:

For –*i* adjectives

atarashii + kirei = atarashi**kute** kirei (*new and clean*)

For –*na* adjectives

benri + yasui = benri **de** yasui (*convenient and cheap*)

## RENSHŪ 1.4

Try connecting the adjectives in the following sentences:

1   Tanaka-san no uchi wa (*big and spacious*) desu.
2   Hiruton Hoteru wa (*spacious and interesting*) desu.
3   Resutoran wa (*clean and cheap*) desu.
4   Nihon ryōri wa (*tasty and expensive*) desu ne!
5   Chikatetsu* wa (*cheap and convenient*) desu.

*Chikatetsu *underground railway*

**KAIWA NI** *Nan-ji kara nan-ji made desu ka*

**Jikan** 5-ji goro
**Basho** Kaisha
**Jinbutsu** Hayashi kachō to Timu Gurosutā

📼 Study these expressions. Then listen to them on cassette and repeat them in the pauses provided.

| | |
|---|---|
| nan-ji | *what time* |
| gogo | *p.m.* |
| shichi-ji | *7.00 (seven o'clock)* |
| ku-ji han | *9.30 (half past nine)* |
| gakkō | *school* |
| Shibuya-eki | *Shibuya Station* |
| . . . ni arimasu | *located (at/in) . . .* |
| demo | *however* |
| . . . kara, . . . | *because* |
| jikan | *the time* |
| daijōbu desu | *it's OK, no problem* |
| chikakute benri desu | *close and convenient* |

📼 Kaiwa ni o kiite kudasai:

HAYASHI: Nihongo no ressun wa kin-yōbi desu ne. Nan-ji kara nan-ji made desu ka.
TIMU: Shichi-ji kara ku-ji han made desu.
HAYASHI: Kaisha wa go-ji han made desu kara, kin-yōbi wa taihen desu ne.
TIMU: Ē, demo gakkō wa Shibuya-eki no mae ni arimasu kara, jikan wa daijōbu desu.
HAYASHI: Shibuya no gakkō desu ka. Sore wa chikakute benri desu ne.

**NARAIMASHŌ**  *Asking the time*

To ask the time, say:

sumimasen, ima nan-ji desu ka    *excuse me, what is the time now?*

*Ima* means 'now'. *Nan-ji* means 'what hour'. You can answer with:

| | |
|---|---|
| ni-ji desu | *it's two o'clock* |
| yo-ji desu | *it's four o'clock (note: not* yon-ji desu*)* |
| shichi-ji desu | *it's seven o'clock* |
| ku-ji desu | *it's nine o'clock (note: not* kyū-ji desu*)* |

To say 'half past', use *han*:

| | |
|---|---|
| ni-ji **han** desu | *it's half past two* |
| yo-ji **han** desu | *it's half past four* |

Remember that a.m. (*gozen*) and p.m. (*gogo*) come before the time they qualify:

| | |
|---|---|
| **gozen** jū-ji han desu | *it's 10.30 a.m.* |
| **gogo** roku-ji desu | *it's 6.00 p.m.* |

---

**RENSHŪ 2.1**

Ima nan-ji desu ka

Practise telling the time in Japanese by saying the times shown below.

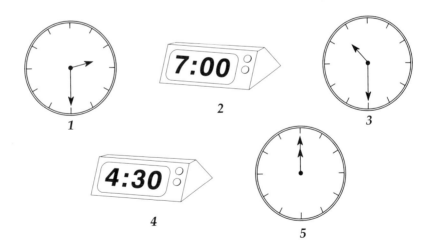

**BUNPŌ**  *Asking where something is located*

To ask where something is located, use the pattern:

| | |
|---|---|
| *'place'* wa doko ni arimasu ka | *where is [the location of] 'place'?* |
| Supōtsu sentā **wa** doko **ni** arimasu ka | *where is the sports centre located?* |

The particle *ni* here means in or at. *Arimasu* in this sentence expresses the location of an inanimate thing (in this case, a sports centre).

| | |
|---|---|
| supōtsu sentā **wa** asoko **ni** arimasu | *the sports centre is over there* |
| kōhiishoppu Maya **wa** Ginza **ni** arimasu | *the coffee-shop Maia is in Ginza* |

In both of the sentences, the place (sports centre, coffee-shop) is the topic of the sentence.

To explain where something is located in relation to another place, use this pattern:

*'thing'* wa *'place'* no *'preposition'* ni arimasu

| | |
|---|---|
| gakkō **wa** Shibuya eki **no** mae **ni** arimasu | *the school is in front of Shibuya station* |
| wa-ei jiten **wa** tēburu **no** ue **ni** arimasu | *the Japanese–English dictionary is on top of the table* |
| yūbinkyoku **wa** hoteru **no** tonari **ni** arimasu | *the post office is located next door to the hotel* |

---

**RENSHŪ 2.2**

Tim is calling a friend to find out a good venue for a get-together. Take turns with a partner to play the part of Tim and his friend by asking and noting down the information. Use the questions provided as a starting point.

Supōtsu Sentā
Itabashi 9 - 31
☎ 285233
8.30am – 11.00pm
Yasumi (Mon)

Resutoram Hana
Yotsuya 1-2-3
Tel: 539123
9.00am – 11.30pm
Yasumi (Wed)

Cafe Minami
Tel: 647392
Harajuku 1 - 7
10.00am - 9.00pm
Yasumi (Thur)

1  ............ wa doko ni arimasu ka.
2  Denwa bangō wa nan-ban desu ka.
3  Nan-ji kara nan-ji made desu ka.
4  Yasumi wa nan-yōbi desu ka.

**RENSHŪ 2.3**

Look at the following picture of Tim's office. Which of the following statements
is true? Tick T or F as appropriate.

                                                    T        F

1  Hon wa tsukue no shita ni arimasu.
2  Wāpuro wa denwa no soba ni arimasu.
3  Fakkusu wa tsukue no ue ni arimasu.
4  Fairu wa fakkusu no mae ni arimasu.
5  Kaban wa isu no ue ni arimasu.

### RENSHŪ 2.4

Tim has just popped into the Personnel Department to ask about facilities in the neighbourhood of his dormitory. Listen to the cassette as Ms Ito from the personnel department points out to Tim where everything is on the map. Label each building with an appropriate letter from the box below.

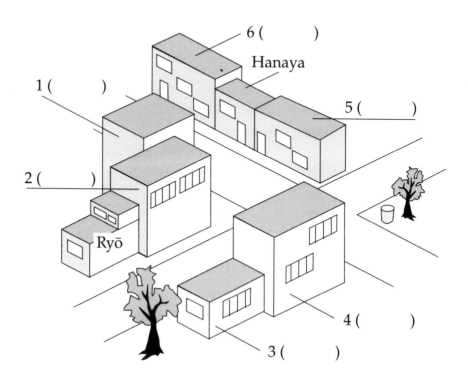

6 (     )

Hanaya

1 (     )

5 (     )

2 (     )

Ryō

4 (     )

3 (     )

| | | |
|---|---|---|
| **a** ginkō | *bank* | |
| **b** yūbinkyoku | *post office* | |
| **c** depāto | *department store* | |
| **d** eki | *station* | |
| **e** sūpā | *supermarket* | |
| **f** supōtsu sentā | *sports club* | |

## KAIWA SAN    *Timu-san, ima kara ryō ni ikimasu ka*

**Jikan**    Gogo 5-ji han
**Basho**    Kaigaikikakubu
**Jinbutsu**  Watanabe-san to Timu Gurosutā

Study these expressions. Then listen to them on cassette and repeat them in the pauses provided.

| | |
|---|---|
| ryō ni ikimasu | *(I'm) going to the dorm* |
| hoteru ni kaerimasu | *(I'm) going back to the hotel* |
| ichi-dō | *once, one time* |
| nan-de | *by what means (of transport)* |
| . . . ka . . . | *. . . or . . .* |
| 55-ban no basu | *the number 55 bus* |
| aruite 5-fun | *a five-minute walk ([by] walking five minutes)* |
| . . . kara, . . . | *because* |
| . . . to issho-ni | *together with . . .* |
| 5-fun kan | *a period of five minutes* |
| 5-fun kan gurai kakarimasu | *it takes about five minutes* |
| dono gurai | *about how long?* |

**NARAIMASHŌ**    *Numbers 10–100*

| | | | |
|---|---|---|---|
| 10 | jū | 20 | ni-jū |
| 11 | jū-ichi | 30 | san-jū |
| 12 | jū-ni | 40 | yon-jū |
| 13 | jū-san | 50 | go-jū |
| 14 | jū-yon | 60 | roku-jū |
| 15 | jū-go | 70 | nana-jū |
| 16 | jū-roku | 80 | hachi-jū |
| 17 | jū-nana/ju-shichi | 90 | kyū-jū |
| 18 | jū-hachi | 100 | hyaku |
| 19 | jū-kyū | | |

Kaiwa san o kiite kudasai:

WATANABE:   Timu-san, ima kara ryō ni ikimasu ka.

TIMU:   Hai, ikimasu. Demo, ichi-do hoteru ni kaerimasu. Hoteru ni kaban ga arimasu kara.

WATANABE:   Sō desu ka. Hoteru kara ryō made nan de ikimasu ka.

TIMU:   Basu de ikimasu.

WATANABE:   Ja, 54-ban ka 55-ban no basu desu ne. Watashi no apāto wa ryō kara aruite go-fun desu kara, watashi wa Timu-san to issho-ni ryō ni ikimasu yo.

TIMU:   A dōmo arigatō . . . Sorede ryō kara kaisha made basu de dono gurai kakarimasu ka.

WATANABE:   Ryō kara kaisha made wa . . . sō desu ne . . . basu de . . . ichi-jikan gurai kakarimasu ne.

TIMU:   Ee?!

**BUNPŌ**    *Presenting information about something in a place*

| | |
|---|---|
| hoteru ni kaban ga arimasu | *in the hotel there is a suitcase (= I've got my suitcase in the hotel)* |

Here the topic of the sentence is the suitcase. It is *new* information to the other person and requires the pattern:

*'place'* ni *'something'* ga arimasu

| | |
|---|---|
| tēburu no shita **ni** o-kane **ga** arimasu | *there's some money under the table (which perhaps you didn't know about)* |
| shachō-shitsu **ni** fakkusu **ga** arimasu | *there's a fax machine in the president's room (I'm telling you about it)* |
| ikkai **ni** kopii-shitsu **ga** arimasu | *on the first floor there is a photocopying room* |

**RENSHŪ 3.1**

Can you describe where the following rooms are on this floor plan of the Japan Industrial branch office in Osaka? To help you, first study these new words:

ikkai *first floor*                    nikai *second floor*                    sangai *third floor*

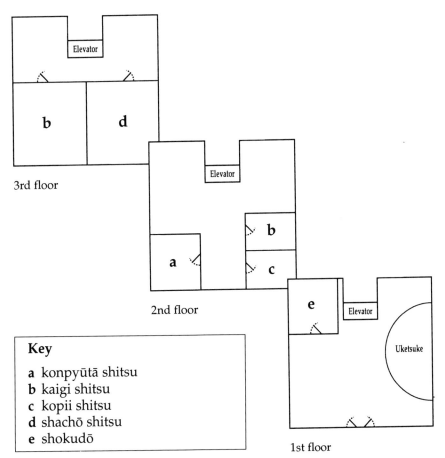

3rd floor

2nd floor

1st floor

**Key**

a konpyūtā shitsu
b kaigi shitsu
c kopii shitsu
d shachō shitsu
e shokudō

Make up questions and answers about the floor plan by following this pattern:

**Rei**   Q: Ikkai ni nani ga arimasu ka.
         A: Ikkai ni shokudō ga arimasu.

1 Q: Nikai ni . . .
   A: . . .
2 Q: Nikai ni . . .
   A: . . .
3 Q: Nikai ni . . .
   A: . . .
4 Q: Sangai ni . . .
   A: . . .
5 Q: Sangai ni . . .
   A: . . .

**NARAIMASHŌ**    *The minutes*

| | | | |
|---|---|---|---|
| 1 | ippun | 9 | kyūfun |
| 2 | nifun | 10 | juppun or jippun |
| 3 | sanpun | 15 | jūgofun |
| 4 | yonpun | 30 | sanjuppun |
| 5 | gofun | 40 | yonjuppun |
| 6 | roppun | 45 | yonjūgofun |
| 7 | nanafun | 50 | gojuppun |
| 8 | happun or hachifun | 55 | gojūgofun |

**RENSHŪ 3.2**

Listen to the cassette to hear the conductor on a *Tōkaidō Sanyō Shinkansen* travelling between Tokyo and Kyoto telling his passengers about the expected arrival times of the train. Fill in the information below, noting that the conductor uses the 24-hour clock i.e. 6.35 p.m. will be 18.35 or *jū-hachi-ji san-jū-go-fun*:

1  Shin Yokohama ni wa . . .

2  Hamamatsu ni wa . . .

3  Maibara ni wa . . .

4  Toyohashi ni wa . . .

5  Mikawa . . .

6  Nagoya . . .

7  Kyōto . . .

**BUNPŌ**    *Saying 'to go' and 'to come back'*

Verbs in Japanese (for example, *ikimasu* 'to go' and *kaerimasu* 'to come back') do not draw a distinction between numbers of people. So *ikimasu* can mean 'I go', 'you go', 'he, she or it goes', 'we go' and 'they go'.

The pattern *'place ni ikimasu* means 'go to "place"'. Destinations must be marked by *ni*:

| | |
|---|---|
| Tōkyō **ni** kaerimasu | *I'm returning to Tokyo* |
| kaisha **ni** ikimasu | *I'm going to the company* |

To make the negative form of these verbs, replace *–masu* with *–masen*:

| | |
|---|---|
| kyō wa kaisha ni iki**masen** | *I'm not going to the company today* |

**NARAIMASHŌ** *Specifying the means of transport*

nan de ikimasu ka                    *how will you go?*

The *nan de* means 'by what means?' Here are some possible answers using the particle *de*:

| | |
|---|---|
| kuruma **de** ikimasu | *go by car* |
| basu **de** ikimasu | *go by bus* |
| takushii **de** ikimasu | *go by taxi* |
| hikōki **de** ikimasu | *go by plane* |
| shinkansen **de** ikimasu | *go by bullet train* |
| densha **de** ikimasu | *go by train* |
| jitensha **de** ikimasu | *go by bicycle* |
| ferii **de** ikimasu | *go by ferry* |
| fune **de** ikimasu | *go by boat* |

Note: 'By foot' or 'on foot' is *aruite ikimasu*, literally, 'by walking-go'.

| | |
|---|---|
| hikōki de Furansu ni ikimasu | *I'm going to France by plane* |
| ashita shinkansen de Sendai ni ikimasu | *I'm going to Sendai tomorrow by bullet train* |

**RENSHŪ 3.3**

Look at the picture below and make up dialogues based on the pattern provided:

**Rei**

A:  Ashita doko ni ikimasu ka.
B:  Ōsaka ni ikimasu.
A:  Nan de ikimasu ka.
B:  Hikōki de ikimasu. Tōkyō kara Ōsaka made hikōki de ichi-ji kan desu.
A:  Itsu kaerimasu ka.
B:  Raishū no kayōbi ni kaerimasu.

**NARAIMASHŌ** *Saying 'go with someone'*

To say 'go with someone', use the pattern: *'person'* to ikimasu.

| | |
|---|---|
| Tomodachi **to** ikimasu | *I'm going with a friend* |
| Morita-san **to** ikimasu | *I'm going with Miss Morita* |

To say 'go by oneself', use: *hitori de ikimasu*.

Tomodachi **to** ikimasu ka          *are you going with friends?*
Iie, **hitori de** ikimasu.          *no, I'm going by myself*

To ask 'who are you going with', say:

**dare to** ikimasu ka               *who are you going with?*

And to ask 'who's going', say:

**dare ga** ikimasu ka               *who's going?*

---

 **RENSHŪ 3.4**

Listen to the three dialogues on the cassette and fill in the missing information below:

1  Mr Hayashi will go to ………. by ………. and return home ………..
2  The secretary is on her way to ………. She's going to go there ………. She'll be back at ………..
3  Watanabe-san and Keiko are going to ………. and their means of transport will be ………. They will meet at around ………. and return at about ………..

**RENSHŪ 3.5**

Here's what Tim is going to do on his first day off. Imagine his conversation with Maki Morita using the following information and words:

**Sukejūru**
9.00    sūpā
10.30   yūbinkyoku
12.00   resutoran
1.30    supōtsu sentā
5.00    ryō

 You can listen to their actual conversation on cassette; compare your version with theirs and then practise what they say with a partner.

NARAIMASHŌ  *Giving a reason for something*

To give a reason for something, use the following pattern with *kara* meaning 'because':

isogashii desu kara, pātii ni ikimasen    *because I'm busy, I'm not going to the party*

gogo go-ji han desu kara, kaerimasu       *it's half past five, so I'm going home (= because it's half past five, I'm going home)*

**RENSHŪ 3.6**

Now Maki Morita is compiling a list of people who will be attending Tim's welcome party. Here is the list:

Watanabe    OK
Tanaka      NG (Kyōto no daiji-na
                 sērusu miitingu.)

Ito         OK
Kosaka      OK
Oba         NG (Kodomo no tanjōbi
                 no pāti.)

Terada      NG (Ōsaka no māketingu
                 kōsu.)

Sakamoto    NG (Nyū Yōku no ofisu.)

She reports this to her boss. What did she say to him about Tanaka, Oba, Terada and Sakamoto? The first excuse is done for you.

1  Tanaka:  Tanaka-san wa Kyōto no daiji-na sērusu miitingu ni ikimasu kara, Timu-san no kangeikai ni kimasen.

2  Oba:

3  Terada:

4  Sakamoto:

**KAIWA YON**  *Nan-ji ni kaisha ni kimasu ka*

**Jikan**     5-ji han goro
**Basho**     Kaigaikikakubu
**Jinbutsu**  Watanabe-san to Timu Gurosutā

Study these expressions. Then listen to them on cassette and repeat them in the pauses provided.

| | |
|---|---|
| kaisha ni kimasu | *come to the company* |
| motto hayai desu | *even earlier* |
| hayaku kaerimasu | *go home early* |
| watashi mo sō deshita | *it was the same for me* |
| deshita | *was* |
| shichi-ji ni | *at seven o'clock* |
| kaerimashita | *I returned* |
| otsukaresama deshita | *well done!* |
| nagakute taihen | *long and tedious* |

Kaiwa yon o kiite kudasai:

TIMU: Watanabe-san, ashita nan-ji ni kaisha ni kimasu ka.
WATANABE: Hachi-ji han goro kimasu.
TIMU: Hayai desu ne.
WATANABE: Kachō wa motto hayai desu yo. Hachi-ji ni kimasu.
TIMU: Hē! Ja, hayaku kaerimasu ka.
WATANABE: Iie. Gogo shichi-ji goro kaerimasu.
TIMU: Ja, kachō no shigoto wa jū-ichi-ji kan desu ne.
WATANABE: Kinō watashi mo sō deshita yo. Kinō no kaigi wa nagakute taihen deshita. Shichi-ji ni kaerimashita.
TIMU: Sore wa taihen deshita ne. Otsukaresama deshita.

---

**BUNPŌ**    *The past tense*

shichi-ji ni kaeri**mashita**    *I went home at seven o'clock*

*Kaerimashita* is the past tense of *kaerimasu* 'to return', 'go home'. To form the past tense, take off the *–masu* part of the verb and replace it with *–mashita*:

| | | | |
|---|---|---|---|
| iki**masu**→ | iki– → | iki**mashita** | *I went* |
| ki**masu**→ | ki– → | ki**mashita** | *I came* |
| tabe**masu**→ | tabe– → | tabe**mashita** | *I ate* |

The past tense of *desu* is *deshita*.

| | |
|---|---|
| Tanaka-san deshita | *it was Miss Tanaka* |
| taihen deshita | *it was awful* |

The negative past tense of desu ('I was not', 'it was not') is *dewa arimasen deshita*. To form the negative of the past tense ('I did not') of other verbs:

| | | | | |
|---|---|---|---|---|
| iki**masu**→ | iki**masen** + | deshita→ | iki**masen** deshita | *I did not go* |
| ki**masu**→ | ki**masen** + | deshita→ | ki**masen** deshita | *I did not come* |
| tabe**masu**→ | tabe**masen** + | deshita→ | tabe**masen** deshita | *I did not eat* |

**NARAIMASHŌ**  Hayaku kaerimasu – *to go home early*

*Hayaku kaerimasu* 'to go home early' features the adverb *hayaku* which is derived from the *–i* adjective *hayai* 'early'. Other adverbs formed by replacing the *–i* with *–ku* are:

| | |
|---|---|
| ōkiku kakimasu | *write it big* (literally, 'bigly' write) |
| chiisaku kakimasu | *write it small* (From *chiisai* 'small', 'little') |
| osoku kaerimasu | *come back late* (From *osoi* 'slow', 'late') |

**RENSHŪ 4.1**

Try to finish the sentences begun on the left by drawing a line to the appropriate endings on the right.

1  Ashita nan-ji ni  
2  Kinō basu de Tōkyō ni  
3  Raishū no kayōbi wa  
4  Kinō nan-ji ni ryō ni  
5  Ashita wa nichiyōbi desu kara  
6  Dare ga  

a  ikimashita.  
b  kimashita ka.  
c  kaisha ni ikimasen.  
d  yūbinkyoku ni ikimasu ka.  
e  Itō-san no kangeikai desu.  
f  kaerimashita ka.  

**NARAIMASHŌ**  *The months of the year*

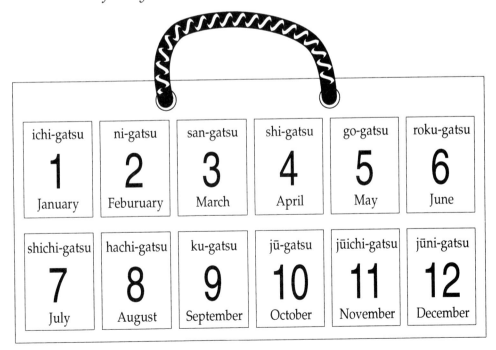

| ichi-gatsu | ni-gatsu | san-gatsu | shi-gatsu | go-gatsu | roku-gatsu |
|---|---|---|---|---|---|
| 1 | 2 | 3 | 4 | 5 | 6 |
| January | Feburuary | March | April | May | June |

| shichi-gatsu | hachi-gatsu | ku-gatsu | jū-gatsu | jūichi-gatsu | jūni-gatsu |
|---|---|---|---|---|---|
| 7 | 8 | 9 | 10 | 11 | 12 |
| July | August | September | October | November | December |

**NARAIMASHŌ**     *The days of the month*

| | | | | |
|---|---|---|---|---|
| 1st | **tsuitachi** | 13th | jū-san-nichi |
| 2nd | **futsuka** | 14th | **jū-yokka** |
| 3rd | **mikka** | 15th | jū-go-nichi |
| 4th | **yokka** | 16th | jū-roku-nichi |
| 5th | **itsuka** | 17th | jū-shichi-nichi |
| 6th | **muika** | 18th | jū-hachi-nichi |
| 7th | **nanoka** | 19th | jū-ku-nichi |
| 8th | **yōka** | 20th | **hatsuka** |
| 9th | **kokonoka** | 21st | ni-jū-ni-nichi |
| 10th | **tōka** | 24th | **ni-jū-yokka** |
| 11th | jū-ichi-nichi | 30th | san-jū-nichi |
| 12th | jū-ni-nichi | 31st | san-jū-ichi-nichi |

Note in particular the dates highlighted!

---

**RENSHŪ 4.2**

This is Tim's schedule for the next month. Listen to the cassette to find out what he is doing on a particular day.

| 日 | 月 | 火 | 水 | 木 | 金 | 土 |
|---|---|---|---|---|---|---|
| 1 | A | 3 | 4 | 5 | 6 | 7 |
| B | 9 | 10 | 11 | 12 | 13 | C |
| 15 | 16 | D | 18 | 19 | 20 | 21 |
| 22 | 23 | 24 | 25 | E | 27 | 28 |
| 29 | 30 | 31 | | | | |

1  ... meeting

2  ... golf

3  ... restaurant

4  ... go to friend's house

**RENSHŪ 4.3**

Maki Morita is organising a list of people who will attend a birthday party (*tanjōbi no pātii*) for Watanabe-san. Study the conversation she has with Tanaka-san, practising it with a partner until you feel confident of all the words and their meanings:

MAKI: Tanaka-san, Watanabe-san no tanjōbi pātii ni kimasu ka.
TANAKA: Itsu desu ka.
MAKI: Shichi-gatsu jū-ni-nichi desu.
TANAKA: Doko desu ka.
MAKI: Horidē In desu.
TANAKA: Hai, ikimasu.

Now make similar conversations for the situations detailed below. Remember that you can choose to say 'Yes, I'm going' (*hai, ikimasu*) or 'No, I'm not going' (*iie, ikimasen*).

1 (Two colleagues, Ito and Sakamoto)
 A sales meeting (*sērusu miitingu*), June 10th, big meeting room.
2 (Two office ladies, Kazuko and Noriko)
 Yumi's birthday party, September 5th, the McDonald's in Sakae.
3 (Two managers, Okamoto and Terada)
 The company president's birthday party, November 19th, the Imperial Hotel (*Teikoku Hoteru*).

## FUKUSHŪ

## FUKUSHŪ 1

How would you say the following in Japanese?

1 I'm going by ferry.
2 Tomorrow I'm going to Yokohama by bus.
3 Next week our manager (*kachō*) is going to Sapporo by plane.
4 I walk to the company.
5 Are you going by taxi?
6 Mr Okamoto goes home by car.
7 I'm going to Canberra (*Kyanbera*) from Sydney (*Shidonii*) by train.
8 Next month Miss Morita is going to Hiroshima by shinkansen.

## FUKUSHŪ 2

Listen to the cassette tape and answer the questions which follow:

1 a Who is – and isn't – coming to the meeting?
 b Why?
2 a When is the taxi coming?
 b Where will it come to?
3 a Who comes to the company first in the morning?
 b What time does that person get in?
4 a When will the Director come back from Germany?
 b When will Miss Watanabe come back?

## FUKUSHŪ 3

Here is a memo on Ueda *buchō*'s desk showing when everyone is having a holiday. Imagine you are the clerk who has to tell Personnel the dates:

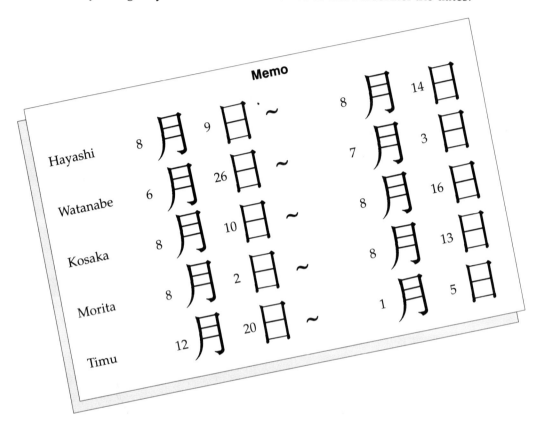

1  Hayashi-san no yasumi wa .......... kara .......... made desu.
2  Watanabe-san no yasumi wa .......... kara .......... made desu.
3  Kosaka-san no yasumi wa .......... kara .......... made desu.
4  Morita-san no yasumi wa .......... kara .......... made desu.
5  Timu-san no yasumi wa .......... kara .......... made desu.

## FUKUSHŪ 4

Make dialogues by changing the prompts into Japanese.

1  Two friends talking.
A:  Resutoran Samurai wa yūmei desu ka.
B:  *No, it is not well-known, but the food is tasty and cheap.*
A:  Ja, watashi no tanjōbi ni Samurai ni ikimasu. Denwa bangō wa nan-ban desu ka.
B:  *The telephone number is 03-754-5891.*

**2**   At the office.

A:   Watanabe-san wa ashita no pātii ni kimasu ka.
B:   *No, Mr Watanabe is not coming to the party.*
A:   Watanabe-san wa isogashii desu ka.
B:   *Yes, Mr Watanabe went on a business trip with Mr Noda yesterday.*


**3**   Looking for the sports centre.

A:   Sumimasen. Supōtsu sentā wa doko ni arimasu ka.
B:   *There is a sports centre in front of the station.*
A:   Koko kara basu de dono gurai kakarimasu ka.
B:   *It takes about 30 minutes.*


**4**   How was the meeting?

A:   Kinō no kaigi wa nan-ji kara nan-ji made deshita ka.
B:   *From 10.00 a.m. to 3.00 p.m.*
A:   Otsukaresama. Taihen deshita ne.
B:   *Yes. The meeting was long and boring (not interesting).*


## FUKUSHŪ 5

Put appropriate particles (such as *ni, no, de, to, wa,* and *ga*) or words (such as *kara* or *made*) in the spaces below. If you don't need to fill one of the blanks, just put an X.

   **1**   Fairu .......... denwa no yoko .......... ni arimasu.
   **2**   Nihongo .......... ressun wa 7-ji kara .......... 9-ji .......... desu.
   **3**   Watashi wa Katō-san .......... resutoran .......... ikimasu.
   **4**   Nagoya ni Shinkansen .......... ikimasu.
   **5**   Kyō nan-ji .......... uchi .......... kaerimasu ka.
   **6**   Watanabe-san .......... pātii .......... kimasu ka.
   **7**   Sangatsu wa Amerika-shutchō .......... arimasu .........., isogashii desu.
   **8**   Ashita wa nichiyōbi desu .........., watashi wa kaisha .......... kimasen.
   **9**   Kaisha wa yūbinkyoku .......... ushiro .......... arimasu.
  **10**   Kore wa benri .......... yasui wāpuro desu.

## FUKUSHŪ 6

Katō-san and Morita-san are talking about Katō-san's forthcoming business trip. Listen to the cassette and tick T or F.

                                                     T        F

   **1**   Mr Katō is going to Osaka.
   **2**   He will go by train.
   **3**   He will go alone.
   **4**   He will go on October 3rd.
   **5**   He will come back on October 8th.

## FUKUSHŪ 7

Rōrupurē

You're in a coffeeshop with a work colleague talking about a business trip that's coming up. Work out the conversation that takes place.

**You**                                                    **Your work colleague**

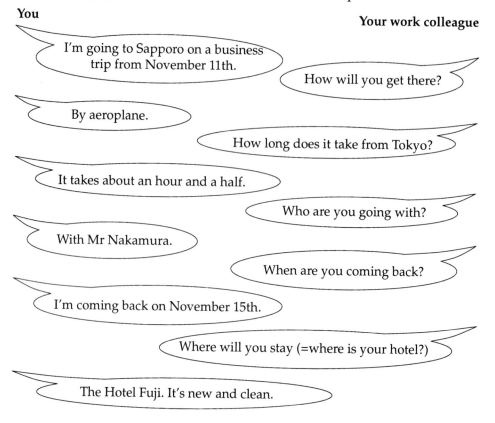

I'm going to Sapporo on a business trip from November 11th.

How will you get there?

By aeroplane.

How long does it take from Tokyo?

It takes about an hour and a half.

Who are you going with?

With Mr Nakamura.

When are you coming back?

I'm coming back on November 15th.

Where will you stay (=where is your hotel?)

The Hotel Fuji. It's new and clean.

# SAIGO NI

Before going on to the next lesson, make sure you can:

| | |
|---|---|
| • ask where something is | *kaisha wa doko ni arimasu ka* |
| • say where places and things are | *kaisha wa eki no mae ni arimasu* |
| • ask how to get somewhere | *nan de ikimasu ka* |
| • ask for a telephone number | *denwa bangō wa nanban desu ka* |
| • understand a telephone number | *denwa bangō wa zero-san-no-yon-hachi-ichi-no kyū-nana-zero desu* |
| • ask the time | *ima nan-ji desu ka* |
| • ask when something is going to happen | *kaigi wa itsu desu ka* |
| • give reasons | *isogashii desu kara, ikimasen* |

# *Mō ichido yukkuri itte kudasai*

## COULD YOU SAY THAT AGAIN MORE SLOWLY?

**In this lesson you will learn how to:**
- receive and make telephone calls
- say you are going somewhere to do something
- use words to describe how often you do something
- take telephone messages
- talk about actions happening now
- ask people to do something for you

**KAIWA ICHI**    *Ima imasen*

**Jikan**    Gozen 10.00
**Basho**    Kaigaikikakubu
**Jinbutsu** Timu Gurosutā to Nihon Denki no Kondō

Study these expressions. Then listen to them on cassette and repeat them in the pauses provided.

| | |
|---|---|
| moshi moshi | *are you there? (telephone expression)* |
| Nihon Denki | *Japan Electric* |
| ima imasen | *he/she is not here at present* |
| gaishutsu-chū | *out of the office* |
| dewa mata | *(I'll call) again* |

Kaiwa ichi o kiite kudasai:

KONDO:  Moshi-moshi.
TIMU:     Hai, kaigaikikakubu no Gurosutā desu ga . . .
KONDO:  Nihon Denki no Kondō desu ga, Ueda buchō o onegai shimasu.
TIMU:     Sumimasen. Ueda wa ima imasen. Gaishutsu-chū desu. Ginkō ni
              ikimashita.
KONDO:  Itsu kaerimasu ka.
TIMU:     Gogo yoji goro desu.
KONDO:  A sō desu ka. Wakarimashita. Dewa mata.

**BUNPŌ**

## *Saying that someone is not there*

Imasen is the present negative form of the verb *imasu* 'to exist' or 'to be at a place'. *Imasu* is used for animate objects such as people and animals. For inanimate objects such as tables, cars and apples, *arimasu* is used.

| | | |
|---|---|---|
| BOYFRIEND: | Keiko-san wa imasu ka. | *Is Keiko there?* |
| FATHER: | Keiko wa imasen. | *Keiko is not here.* |
| | | |
| GIRLFRIEND: | Kuruma wa arimasu ka. | *Do you have a car?* |
| BOYFRIEND: | Arimasen. | *No.* |

**NARAIMASHŌ**

## *'in the middle of something'*

gaishutsu-chū desu          *he's out at the moment (literally; in the middle of
                                             going out)*

This is a polite way of saying that someone is unavailable. The suffix *–chū* means 'in the middle of' and is used in a variety of useful ways:

| | |
|---|---|
| kaigi-chū | *in the middle of a meeting* |
| denwa-chū | *in the middle of a telephone conversation* |
| hanashi-chū | *in the middle of talking* |
| shokuji-chū | *in the middle of a meal* |
| shutchō-chū | *in the middle of a business trip* |

**RENSHŪ 1.1**

Listen to the five short dialogues on the cassette. Complete the table from the information in the dialogues:

| | 1 | 2 | 3 | 4 | 5 |
|---|---|---|---|---|---|
| Person or organisation calling | | | | | |
| Person to whom he/she wishes to speak | | | | | |

**RENSHŪ 1.2**

Maki Morita has some important memos to hand over to various people. Listen to Maki as she asks questions about where each person is at the moment. Then match each person to the appropriate location.

1  Tim
2  Katō
3  Hayashi-buchō
4  Morita

a  konpyūtā-shitsu
b  kopii-shitsu
c  kyūkei-shitsu
d  shachō-shitsu
e  shokudō

**RENSHŪ 1.3**

a  Look at the pictures and give the reason the person cannot come to the phone:

2 shokuji-chū

1 kaigi-chū

3 shutchō-chū

**b** Imagine you are an OL at Japan Industrial. Make up a dialogue for each of the pictures below, following the pattern of the dialogue below. (There are some prompts to help you along.)

A: Moshi-moshi. Watashi, Sony no Kimura desu ga, Nakamura-buchō o onegai shimasu.
B: Sumimasen ga, Nakamura wa ima imasen. Shutchō-chū desu ga . . .
A: A sō desu ka. Itsu kaerimasu ka.
B: Raishū no suiyōbi ni kaerimasu.
A: A sō desu ka. Wakarimashita. Dewa mata . . .

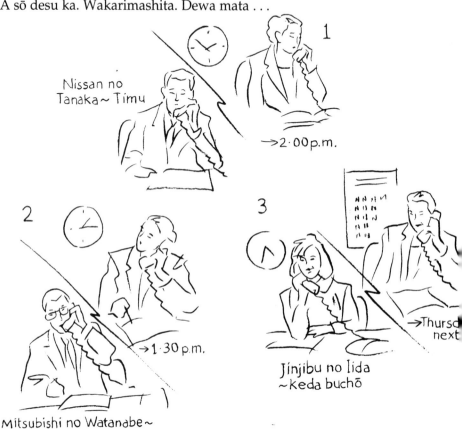

Nissan no Tanaka ~ Timu

1

→2·00p.m.

2

→1·30 p.m.

Mitsubishi no Watanabe ~ Morita Maki

3

→Thursd
next

Jinjibu no Iida
~keda buchō

---

**BUNPŌ** *Summary table of some basic verbs and tenses*

Familiarise yourself with the following:

| –masu form (infinitive) | negative present | past | negative past |
|---|---|---|---|
| ikimasu (*to go*) | ikimasen | ikimashita | ikimasen deshita |
| tabemasu (*to eat*) | tabemasen | tabemashita | tabemasen deshita |
| mimasu (*to see*) | mimasen | mimashita | mimasen deshita |
| hanashimasu (*to speak*) | hanashimasen | hanashimashita | hanashimasen deshita |
| iimasu (*to say*) | iimasen | iimashita | iimasen deshita |
| kikimasu (*to hear*) | kikimasen | kikimashita | kikimasen deshita |
| shimasu (*to do*) | shimasen | shimashita | shimasen deshita |
| kimasu (*to come*) | kimasen | kimashita | kimasen deshita |

**RENSHŪ 1.4**

Look at the pictures below and decide where some of the staff of Japan Industrial went over the O-bon festival during the month of August.

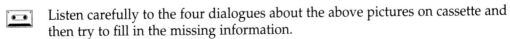

Listen carefully to the four dialogues about the above pictures on cassette and then try to fill in the missing information.

1  Mr Hayashi's trip to Hawaii is from .......... to ........... He went to Hawaii with ...........

2  Mrs Nomura went to play tennis on .......... from .......... o'clock to .......... o'clock.

3  Mr Kida went cycling on .......... (day) with .......... .......... (whom). He returned home at .......... o'clock.

4  Miss Noguchi went to .......... (whose) party. She returned home by ..........

**RENSHŪ 1.5**

It is as important to be able to say that something didn't happen as much as it is to say something did. Here is something that Ueda *buchō* said to his friend Nakamura-san:

senshū gorufu ni ikimashita ga, *last week I went golfing, but this week I*
   konshū wa ikimasen deshita    *didn't go*

Can you complete the following so that they make sense?

1 Kinō watashi wa pātii ni ikimashita ga, Nakamura-san wa ...........

2 Kinō buchō wa pātii ni kimashita ga, shachō wa ...........

3 Kotoshi watashi wa Nihon ni kaerimashita ga, kyonen wa ...........

**KAIWA NI**    *Kōhii o nomimasu*

**Jikan**     Asa no yasumi jikan (*during the morning break*)
**Basho**    Kyūkei-shitsu (*the tea-break room*)
**Jinbutsu** Morita-san to Timu-san

Study these expressions. Then listen to them on cassette and repeat them in the pauses provided.

| | |
|---|---|
| kōhii o nomimasu | *drink coffee* |
| . . . ga arimasen | *there is no . . .* |
| tokidoki | *sometimes* |
| sandoitchi o kaimasu | *buy a sandwich* |
| kai ni ikimasu | *go to buy* |
| ii desu | *it's OK, it's all right* |
| issho ni | *together with (someone)* |

Kaiwa ni o kiite kudasai:

MORITA: Timu-san, nani o nomimasu ka.
TIMU:    Nani ga arimasu ka.
MORITA: Kōhii to kōcha to Nihoncha ga arimasu.
TIMU:    Ja, kōhii o nomimasu.
MORITA: A, miruku ga arimasen.
TIMU:    Ii desu yo. Watashi wa tokidoki burakku kōhii o nomimasu kara.
MORITA: Sumimasen. Hiru yasumi ni miruku o kai ni ikimasu.
TIMU:    Ja, watashi no issho ni ikimasu. Watashi wa sandoitchi o kaimasu.

**BUNPŌ**    *Direct object marker o*

Look at the following sentences:

kōhii o nomimasu                 *I'll drink coffee*
banana o tabemasu                *I'll eat a banana*

Note that the thing which is drunk or eaten is marked by *o*.
This *o* is a direct object marker. Here are some other examples:

nihongo o hanashimasu            *I speak Japanese (the thing I speak is*
                                 *Japanese)*
rajio o kikimasu                 *I listen to the radio (the thing I listen to is*
                                 *the radio)*

**RENSHŪ 2.1**

One of the tedious jobs of an office lady is to remember who drinks what –
whether beer, sake or wine, or all three – as well as how they like their teas and
coffees. Imagine you are eavesdropping on a conversation at Nihon Kōgyō
about drinking preferences. Listen to the cassette and write down what you
think each person drinks:

1  Hayashi

2  Katō

3  Timu

4  Morita

Jūsu

Wain

Bīru

### RENSHŪ 2.2

Some of Tim's prospective clients need to know about how extensive the Japan Industrial (Nihon Kōgyō or NK) operation is and where it fits into the *keiretsu* (industrial conglomerate) to which it belongs. Look at the chart which Tim's *sempai* (senior) Kosaka-san gave him and (as Tim has to do) work out the answers to the questions:

| | Hiroshima | Ōsaka | Kyōto | Nagoya | Tōkyō |
|---|---|---|---|---|---|
| Nihon Kōgyō | | □ | □ | | ○ |
| Nihon Denki | □ | ○ | □ | □ | |
| Nihon Kagaku | | ○ | | | □ |
| Nihon Tsūshō | □ | ○ | | | |

**Key:** Honsha ○
Shisha □

1 Kyōto ni Nihon Kōgyō no shisha ga arimasu ka.
2 Nagoya ni Nihon Denki no shisha ga arimasu ka.
3 Tōkyō ni Nihon Kōgyō no honsha ga arimasu ka.
4 Doko ni Nihon Denki no honsha ga arimasu ka.
5 Kyōto ni Nihon Kagaku no shisha ga arimasu ka.
6 Hiroshima ni Nihon Tsūshō no honsha ga arimasu ka.

### RENSHŪ 2.3

As Tim's week progresses, he begins to absorb more and more new words to enable him to work more effectively. Here are some words which he has memorised: see whether you can absorb them too. First of all, look at the words in the box on the right-hand side. Then try to link them with an appropriate word from the box on the left-hand side. Follow this example:

tenisu o shimasu *play tennis (literally: do tennis)*

| | |
|---|---|
| namae | hon |
| nyūsu | suraido |
| sandoitchi | piza |
| terebi | repōto |
| rajio | gorufu |

| | |
|---|---|
| kakimasu | *to write* |
| mimasu | *to see* |
| shimasu | *to do* |
| tabemasu | *to eat* |
| kikimasu | *to listen* |
| yomimasu | *to read* |

**BUNPŌ** — *How to say 'I'll go and . . .'*

miruku o kai ni ikimasu          *I'll go and buy some milk*

The *kai* here is the stem of the verb *kaimasu* 'to buy'. The pattern stem + *ni ikimasu* means 'to go and do X'. Here are some other examples:

'ET' o mi ni ikimasu          *I'm going to see 'ET'*
(From *mimasu* 'to see')

| | |
|---|---|
| biiru o nomi ni ikimashita | *I went to drink some beer* <br> (From *nomimasu* 'to drink') |
| yakitori o tabe ni ikimasu ka | *would you like to go out for grilled chicken?* <br> (From *tabemasu* 'to eat') |

This stem + *ni* construction can be used with verbs other than *ikimasu* as long as they involve motion:

| | |
|---|---|
| purezentēshon o shi ni kimashita | *I came to do a presentation* |
| terebi nyūsu o mi ni ryō ni kaerimashita | *I went back to the dorm to see the news on TV* |

## RENSHŪ 2.4

Now listen to the cassette and try to match the activity with the person.

| | |
|---|---|
| Morita | go to play tennis. |
| Hayashi | go to make a telephone call. |
| Ueda | go to buy a book. |
| Kimura | go to eat French food. |
| Tim | go to see a film. |
| | go to listen to a concert. |

**NARAIMASHŌ** *Saying how often you do something*

To express how often something happens use the pattern:

frequency word + noun + *o* + verb

tokidoki burakku kōhii o nomimasu    *from time to time I drink black coffee*

Here are some important frequency words:

| | | | |
|---|---|---|---|
| itsumo | *always* | mainichi | *every day* |
| yoku | *often* | maishū | *every week* |
| tokidoki | *sometimes* | maishū kayōbi ni | *every Tuesday* |

## RENSHŪ 2.5

Tim is having a coffee with Katō-san. They are chatting about how often they do certain things. Put the jumbled-up words below into order to make logical sentences. Then write down who you think said the sentence: Tim or Katō-san.

1  Yoku o shimbun no yomimasu eigo
2  Watashi maishū ni wa suiyōbi no nihongo kurasu ikimasu ni
3  Hito kaisha to gorufu no shimasu tokidoki o
4  Issho-ni waifu to maishū doyobi o shi ikimasu kaimono ni depatō ni

## KAIWA SAN   *Matte kudasai*

**Jikan**      Gogo san-ji goro
**Basho**      Kaigaikikakubu
**Jinbutsu**   Timu-san to onna no hito (*Tim and a woman*)

Study these expressions. Then listen to them on cassette and repeat them in the
pauses provided.

| | |
|---|---|
| kono mama | *as it is* |
| machimasu | *wait for someone or something* |
| owarimasu | *to finish* |
| mada owarimasen | *hasn't/isn't finished yet* |
| owarimashita | *is finished* |
| ato de | *afterwards* |
| jōzu ni Nihongo o hanashimasu | *speaks Japanese well* |

Kaiwa san o kiite kudasai:

| | |
|---|---|
| TIMU: | A, moshi-moshi Nihon Kōgyō no Timu Gurosutā desu ga, hambai bu no Nagano-san o onegai shimasu. |
| ONNA NO HITO: | Nagano wa ima denwa-chū desu ga. |
| TIMU: | Ja, kono mama machimasu . . . |
| ONNA NO HITO: | . . . Sumimasen, mada owarimasen. |
| TIMU: | Sō desu ka. Mata ato de denwa o shimasu. |
| ONNA NO HITO: | A, chotto matte kudasai. Ima owarimashita. Nagano-san, Nihon Kogyō no Timu Gurosutā-san kara o-denwa desu. (*Whispering to Yumi, another telephonist*) Yumi-san, Gurosutā-san wa jōzu ni Nihongo o hanashimasu ne. |

**RENSHŪ 3.1**

Maki Morita spends a good deal of her time explaining to callers that the person they wish to speak with is unavailable. Listen to Maki on cassette as she explains where people are. Match the person with the reason he or she is unavailable:

| | | | |
|---|---|---|---|
| 1 | Hayashi | a | at a meeting |
| 2 | Mori | b | on a business trip |
| 3 | Kida | c | at lunch |
| 4 | Kimura | d | on the phone |
| 5 | Satō | e | has a day off |
| | | f | will come to the office this afternoon |

**BUNPŌ**

## *Saying that something is not yet finished*

*Mada* plus the *–masen* form of the verb is the pattern to use to indicate that an action has not yet been completed. Here are some examples:

| | |
|---|---|
| Watashi wa mada shirimasen | *I don't know yet* (from *shirimasu* 'to know a fact') |
| mada shimasen yo | *we're not doing that yet, you know* (from *shimasu* 'to do') |

When *mada* is used in an affirmative sentence it means 'still':

| | |
|---|---|
| Tanaka-san wa **mada** biiru o nonde imasu | *Tanaka's still drinking beer* |
| watashi wa **mada** Nihongo o benkyō shite imasu! | *I'm still studying Japanese!* |

*Mada desu* simply means 'not yet'.

**RENSHŪ 3.2**

Sometimes Maki Morita finds herself playing for time when a caller rings back and the person he or she wishes to talk to is still unavailable. Look at this exchange between Maki and an anxious caller

| | | |
|---|---|---|
| CALLER: | Mō kaigi wa owarimashita ka | *Has the meeting finished yet?* |
| MAKI: | Iie, mada owarimasen | *No, it hasn't finished yet.* |

Maki could also say: *iie, mada desu* 'no, not yet'. If the meeting has in fact already finished, Maki would say: *hai, mō owarimashita*.
To practise this, look at the pictures overleaf. Make up five exchanges to match each situation, using *mō* (already) and *mada desu* (not yet).

1 kaigi
2 purezenteshon
3 denwa
4 hanashi
5 taipu

### RENSHŪ 3.3

Tim has a frustrating day trying to contact various people at different companies. On the right are some of the reasons he was given for why he could not speak to the relevant individual. How might Tim have responded? Choose an appropriate follow-up question to the excuse given.

**Excuse**

1  shutchō-chū desu
2  denwa-chū desu
3  gaishutsu-chū desu
4  kyō wa yasumi desu
5  kaigi-chū desu

**Follow-up questions**

a  nan-ji ni owarimasu ka.
b  kono mama machimasu.
c  ashita kaisha ni kimasu ka.
d  ja, mata ato de denwa shimasu.
e  nan-nichi ni kaerimasu ka.
f  nan-ji goro kaerimasu ka.

**BUNPŌ**    *More information on adverbs*

namae o ōkiku kirei-ni kaite kudasai        *please write your name large and clear*

*Kirei-ni* is an adverb derived from the adjective *kirei-na* 'beautiful, clean'. Some adverbs are formed from –*i* adjectives and others from –*na* adjectives. Adverbs derived from –*na* adjectives add –*ni*:

shizuka desu→shizuka **ni** hanashimasu
*is quiet*        →*talk quietly*

**RENSHŪ 3.4**

Make some statements about the people working at Japan Industrial by selecting an adverb from the middle column and matching it with a phrase from the right column.

| | | | | | |
|---|---|---|---|---|---|
| 1 | Hayashi-san wa | **a** jōzu-ni | | **u** | ranchi o tabemasu |
| 2 | Tim-san wa | **b** hayaku | | **v** | Eigo o hanashimasu |
| 3 | Morita-san wa | **c** osoku | | **w** | Nihongo o kakimasu |
| 4 | Watanabe-san wa | **d** jōzu-ni | | **x** | kaisha ni kimasu |
| 5 | Tanaka-san wa | **e** hayaku | | **y** | kanji o kakimasu |
| 6 | Iida-san wa | **f** kirei-ni | | **z** | uchi ni kaerimasu |

**BUNPŌ**

## Asking someone to do something

*Denwa o shite kudasai* 'please call' (*telephone*) is derived from the verb *denwa [o] shimasu* 'to make a telephone call'. The *kudasai* part means 'please', and is used with a structure called the –*te* form of the verb to make a request of a person to do something. Here are examples of –*te* forms of some verbs which you have met already, plus *kudasai*:

| –*masu* form | –*te* form plus *kudasai* | **English** |
|---|---|---|
| tabemasu | tabete kudasai | *please eat* |
| shimasu | shite kudasai | *please do* |
| kimasu | kite kudasai | *please come* |
| mimasu | mite kudasai | *please look* |
| hanashimasu | hanashite kudasai | *please speak, talk, say* |
| machimasu | matte kudasai | *please wait* |
| ikimasu | itte kudasai | *please go* |
| kikimasu | kiite kudasai | *please listen* |
| kakimasu | kaite kudasai | *please write* |

**RENSHŪ 3.5**

Hayashi *kachō* spends a lot of time asking people to do things. Work out what requests he made today by linking the phrases on the left with those on the right.

| | | | |
|---|---|---|---|
| 1 | Hayaku . . . | **a** | mite kudasai |
| 2 | Heya o kirei ni . . . | **b** | matte kudasai |
| 3 | Shizuka ni . . . | **c** | tabete kudasai |
| 4 | Terebi no oto* o ōkiku . . . | **d** | kite kudasai |
| 5 | Ashita mata . . . | **e** | shite kudasai |
| 6 | Ato sanjuppun . . . | **f** | hanashite kudasai |

*oto *sound, volume*

## RENSHŪ 3.6

Now imagine you're in charge of a Japanese office. How would you give the following orders? The words you will need are shown below:

hanashite          shite          shite          kaite          shite

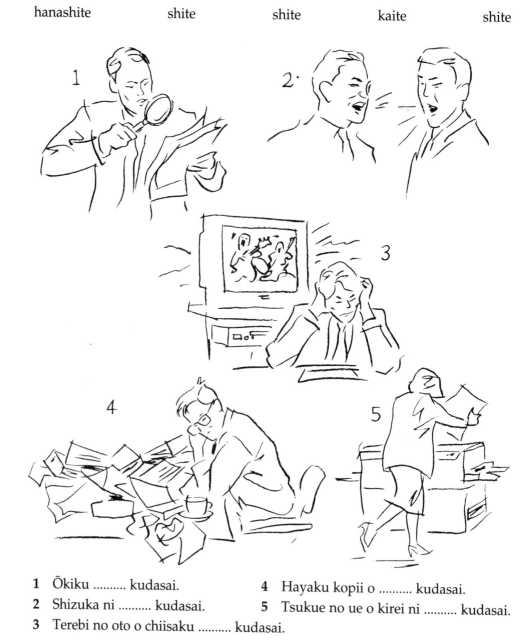

1  Ōkiku .......... kudasai.
2  Shizuka ni .......... kudasai.
3  Terebi no oto o chiisaku .......... kudasai.

4  Hayaku kopii o .......... kudasai.
5  Tsukue no ue o kirei ni .......... kudasai.

## KAIWA YON — *Shachō to hanashi o shite imasu*

**Jikan**     Gogo yoji goro
**Basho**     Kaigaikikakubu
**Jinbutsu**  Timu-san to Nihon Denki no Kondō-san

Study these expressions. Then listen to them on the cassette and repeat in the pauses provided.

| | |
|---|---|
| kaigishitsu de | *in the meeting room* |
| hanashi | *talk, talking* |
| . . . o shite imasu | *is doing . . . (at present)* |
| . . . ni tsutaete kudasai | *please tell (that person)* |
| mō ichido | *once more* |
| yukkuri | *slowly* |
| kyū-na kaigi | *a sudden, unexpected meeting* |
| itte kudasai | *please say, speak* |

Kaiwa yon o kiite kudasai:

KONDO: Nihon Denki no Kondō desu ga, Ueda-buchō wa gaishutsu kara kaerimashita ka.

TIMU: Hai, chotto matte kudasai. Ano sumimasen. Ueda wa ima kaigishitsu de shachō to hanashi o shite imasu.

KONDO: Dewa, Ueda-buchō ni tsutaete kudasai. Ashita no yakusoku wa jūji deshita ga . . .

TIMU: Hai.

KONDO: Anō- kyū na kaigi ga arimasu kara, ashita no asa wa chotto isogashii desu. Ashita no gogo wa ikaga desu ka.

TIMU: Sumimasen. Mō ichido yukkuri itte kudasai.

KONDO: Sā . . .

## BUNPŌ

### *Talking about something happening now or continuously*

Furenchi furai o tabete imasu     *he's eating French fries.*

The verb form *tabete imasu* is roughly equivalent to the English 'is eating': in other words it describes an action or activity which is taking place now or continuously. It is called the 'present continuous tense' and is formed by taking the *–te* form of the verb plus *imasu*. Here are examples of some verbs in the *–te* form with *imasu*:

| *–masu* form | *–te* form plus *imasu* | English |
|---|---|---|
| nomimasu | nonde imasu | *is drinking* |
| tabemasu | tabete imasu | *is eating* |
| shimasu | shite imasu | *is doing* |
| kimasu | kite imasu | *is coming* |
| mimasu | mite imasu | *is looking* |
| hanashimasu | hanashite imasu | *is speaking* |
| machimasu | matte imasu | *is waiting* |
| kikimasu | kiite imasu | *is listening* |
| kakimasu | kaite imasu | *is writing* |

| | |
|---|---|
| Nihongo o benkyō shite imasu | *I'm studying Japanese* |
| terebi o mite imasu | *I'm watching TV right now* |
| Morita-san wa robii de matte imasu yo | *Miss Morita's waiting in the lobby right now you know* |

**RENSHŪ 4.1**

Tim has been asked by Hayashi *kachō* to gather everyone together for an emergency meeting. He asks Maki Morita whether she knows where everyone might be. Look at the pictures and think up questions that Tim might ask and Maki's replies to them i.e. about where the people are and what they are doing:

Ms Watanabe
shachō-shitsu
1. Mr. Iida
kyūkei shitsu
2. Mr. Kosaka
shiryō-shitsu
3. Mr. Terada
kompyūtā shitsu
4. Mr. Murata
uketsuke
5. Mr. Suzuki
kaigishitsu

**Rei**

1  TIMU:  Watanabe-san wa doko ni imasu ka.
   MAKI:  Shachō-shitsu ni imasu.
2  TIMU:  Nani o shite imasu ka.
   MAKI:  Hanashi o shite imasu.

## NARAIMASHŌ  *Action happening at a location*

Rather than *ni, de* is used when there is an action taking place in a given location i.e. drinking coffee in the rest area.

| | |
|---|---|
| kyūkeishitsu de kōhii o nonde imasu | *he's drinking coffee in the rest area* |
| shachō-shitsu de shachō to hanashi o shite imasu | *he's talking to the president in the president's room* |
| imōto wa Ōsaka de Nihongo o benkyō shite imasu | *my younger sister is studying Japanese in Osaka* |

### RENSHŪ 4.2

Having learned from Maki Morita where everyone is and what they are doing, Tim can report back to Hayashi *kachō*. Use the following pattern to work out what Tim said to him:

Watanabe-san wa shachō-shitsu de hanashi o shite imasu

*Miss Watanabe is talking in the president's office*

1  Iida san . . .

2  Kosaka san . . .

3  Terada san . . .

4  Murata san . . .

5  Suzuki san . . .

### RENSHŪ 4.3

Imagine you are a fly on the wall at Japan Industrial. How would you describe what everyone is doing at the moment? (Remember to use *–te imasu* form of the verb in your answers.)

1  Timu-san wa ima denwa o . . .
2  Murata-san wa repōto o . . .
3  Komori-san wa Kida-san to hanashi o . . .
4  Ueda-san wa . . .
5  Kimura-san wa repōto o . . .
6  Morita-san wa fairu o . . .

## RENSHŪ 4.4

Now listen to the cassette. You will hear a series of statements. Looking at your picture of people at work at Japan Industrial, say whether the statements are true or false by ticking T or F.

|   | T | F |   | T | F |
|---|---|---|---|---|---|
| 1 |   |   | 4 |   |   |
| 2 |   |   | 5 |   |   |
| 3 |   |   | 6 |   |   |

## FUKUSHŪ

## FUKUSHŪ 1

Try to answer these questions on the four main *kaiwa* in this chapter.

1  Ueda buchō wa nanji ni ginkō kara kaerimasu ka.
2  Timu-san wa itsumo burakku kōhii o nomimasu ka.
3  Morita-san wa hiru yasumi ni doko ni ikimasu ka.
4  Timu-san wa hiru, nani o tabemasu ka.
5  Kondō-san wa Ueda buchō to hanashimashita ka.
6  Ueda buchō to Kondō-san no yakusoku wa nanji deshita ka.
7  Kondō-san wa ashita no niji goro isogashii desu ka.

## FUKUSHŪ 2

Complete the dialogues below in Japanese using the English prompts. They all take place in the office.

**1**

A: *Are you busy at the moment?*
B: Iie.
A: *Sorry, but could you make copies?*

**2**

A: *Where did you go yesterday?*
B: Ueda buchō to gorufu ni ikimashita.
A: *Do you often play golf?*
B: Un. Maishū nichiyōbi ni gorufu o shimasu.

**3**

A:  Hayashi-san wa mō kaerimashita ka.
B:  *No, he is reading a newspaper in the little meeting room.*
A:  A, so desu ka.
B:  *He always goes home at half past seven.*


## FUKUSHŪ 3

Rearrange the following sentences to make a dialogue between a boss and a secretary:

1  Wakarimashita, ja yoji goro mō ikkai kimasu.

2  Itsu owarimasu ka.

3  Sumimasen, ima taipu o shite imasu.

4  Hai, onegai shimasu.

5  Sō desu ne. Ato ni-ji kan gurai matte kudasai.

6  Taipu wa mō owarimashita ka.

(Hint: start with **6**)


## FUKUSHŪ 4

**a** Here's a copy of a memo Tim has written to himself (it's in a jumble of Japanese and English). If he had written full sentences instead of just short notes, what would the full sentences have been? The first one has been done for you:

**Memo**

1  10:30 am  mr Ochi ni denwa
2  Kato-san  tegami  write
3  Message  from Nakano  tell  personnel
4  4:30 pm  Nakamura-san  aimasu
5  Kyoto shisha  Fax o  okurimasu

**Rei**
1  Gozen jū-ji han mi Ochi-san ni denwa o shimasu.

**b** Imagine that Hayashi kachō had in fact ordered Tim to do these things. How would he have said them? Again, the first one is done for you:

**Rei**
1  Gozen jū-ji han ni Ochi-san ni denwa o shite kudasai.

**NARAIMASHŌ**   *Saying 'tell someone', 'telephone someone'*

| | |
|---|---|
| Ueda kachō **ni** messeji o tsutaete kudasai | *please tell the message (to) Ueda kachō* |
| Mikiko-san **ni** denwa o shite kudasai | *please telephone [to] Mikiko* |

The verb *tsutaemasu* 'to tell', 'inform' (here in its –*te* form with *kudasai*) takes the indirect object marker *ni*, literally 'tell something to someone'. Note the following:

| | |
|---|---|
| watashi wa Nihonjin **ni** Eigo o oshiemasu | *I teach Japanese people English (Lit. I teach English to Japanese people)* |
| jinji-bu **ni** Tanaka-san no denwa bangō o oshiete kudasai | *please tell (to) Personnel Mr Tanaka's telephone number* |

### FUKUSHŪ 5

At the end of the day, Hayashi *kachō* checks to see whether Tim has managed to get through everything he was asked to do today. Listen to the cassette and write against this checklist how far he has progressed with each task.

1  Phone Ochi-san:

2  Letter to Katō-san:

3  Message from Personnel:

4  Meeting with Nakamura:

5  Fax to Kyoto:

### FUKUSHŪ 6

Listen to the following conversations on cassette and then answer the questions.

1  **a** Did Mr Nakano come to the English class last week?
   **b** How often does Mr Nakano go on a business trip?

2  **a** What is Tim doing?
   **b** Is he alone?

3  **a** Why is Mr Hayashi not available on the phone?
   **b** What does the telephone caller say?

4  **a** Where is Miss Morita, and what is she doing now?
   **b** What is Mr Nakano going to do?

5  **a** Who was the caller?
   **b** What was his message?

### FUKUSHŪ 7

How would you say the following in Japanese?

1  Can I speak to Mr Nakano?

2  Please wait a minute.

3  I'm sorry.

4 Mr Hayashi is having a meeting now.

5 The meeting has not finished yet.

6 Please speak slowly.

7 I'll telephone back later.

8 When will Mr Hayashi return from his business trip?

9 I came to the office at 7.00 yesterday.

10 I often eat lunch at the company canteen.

## FUKUSHŪ 8

Rōrupurē

You are about to receive a telephone call from Mr Tanaka. It's around 9.45 a.m. Take turns with a partner to practise both sides of the conversation.

**You**                                                    **Mr Tanaka, the caller**

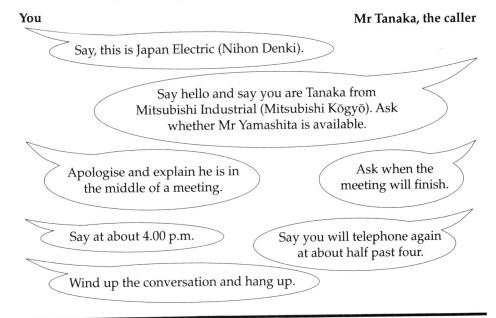

Say, this is Japan Electric (Nihon Denki).

Say hello and say you are Tanaka from Mitsubishi Industrial (Mitsubishi Kōgyō). Ask whether Mr Yamashita is available.

Apologise and explain he is in the middle of a meeting.

Ask when the meeting will finish.

Say at about 4.00 p.m.

Say you will telephone again at about half past four.

Wind up the conversation and hang up.

# SAIGO NI

Before you move on to the next lesson, make sure you can:

| | |
|---|---|
| • ask for someone on the phone | *Tanaka-san onegai shimasu* |
| • say that someone is not in the office at the moment | *ima gaishutsu-chū desu* |
| • say you will telephone back later | *dewa mata ato de denwa o shimasu* |
| • request someone to repeat more slowly what they just said | *mō ichido yukkuri itte kudasai* |
| • ask someone to make copies | *kopii o shite kudasai* |
| • say what is happening at the moment | *ima kōhii o nonde imasu* |

# *Taihen omoshirokatta desu*

## IT WAS REALLY INTERESTING

> **In this lesson you will learn how to:**
> • **buy train tickets, food and drink**
> • **start using the Japanese counting systems**
> • **talk about wanting to do something**
> • **give directions**
> • **learn some standard apologies**

**KAIWA ICHI** *Ōsaka made ōfuku ni-mai kudasai*

**Jikan**     Gozen 9.30
**Basho**    Shinkansen kippu uriba
**Jinbutsu** Timu to kippu uriba no hito

Study these expressions. Then listen to them on cassette and repeat them in the pauses provided.

| | |
|---|---|
| ōfuku | *return (ticket)* |
| jiyūseki | *non-reserved seat* |
| shiteiseki | *reserved seat* |
| katamichi | *single (ticket)* |
| ikura | *how much?* |
| ¥56000 (go-man roku sen en) | *56000 yen* |
| tsugi no shinkansen | *the next bullet train* |
| hayaku tsukimasu | *arrives early* |

Kaiwa ichi o kiite kudasai:

| | |
|---|---|
| TIMU: | Ōsaka made ōfuku ni-mai kudasai. |
| KIPPU URIBA NO HITO: | Jiyūseki desu ka. |
| TIMU: | Iie, shiteiseki o onegai shimasu. |
| KIPPU URIBA NO HITO: | Nan-ji no shinkansen desu ka. |
| TIMU: | Tsugi no shinkansen wa nanji desu ka. |
| KIPPU URIBA NO HITO: | 9.50 desu ga, Ōsaka ni wa 10.15 no hō ga hayaku tsukimasu. |
| TIMU: | Dewa, 10.15 no densha de ikimasu. Zenbu de ikura desu ka. |
| KIPPU URIBA NO HITO: | ¥56000 desu. |
| TIMU: | Purattohōmu wa nan-ban desu ka. |
| KIPPU URIBA NO HITO: | 14-ban desu. |

**NARAIMASHŌ**

## *The unit* man *(10000)*

Japanese uses *man* (10000) as a unit for counting large numbers.

ichi man en *one ten thousand yen* = ¥10000
san man go-sen en *three ten thousands, and five thousand yen* = ¥35000
jū-man en *ten ten thousands yen* = ¥100000
jū-go man en *fifteen ten thousands yen* = ¥150000
jūhachi man roku-sen en *eighteen ten thousands, and six thousand yen* = ¥186000

Note also: *oku* is the word for 'a hundred million' (*ichi oku en* 'one hundred million yen'), *chō* is the word for 'a billion' (*itchō en* 'one billion yen').

**RENSHŪ 1.1**

Tim went shopping for a new camera during his visit to Osaka. On the way he saw various items on sale. How did he report what bargains he saw to Maki Morita? Look at the example to help you along.

**Rei**   Konpyūtā wa jū-sanman-en (¥130000) deshita ga, ima jū-ichiman-en (¥110000) desu. Ni-man-en (¥20000) yasui desu.

konpyūtā   ¥130,000   ¥110,000

kuruma   ¥950,000   ¥760,000

yubiwa   ¥240,000   ¥180,000

kamkōdā   ¥120,000   ¥90,000

kamera   ¥16,000   ¥7,000

pen   ¥59,000   ¥39,000

---

**BUNPŌ**   *Using Japanese counters*

Ōsaka made ōfuku ni-mai kudasai        *two returns to Osaka please*

The full sentence here is: *Ōsaka made ōfuku **kippu** o ni-mai kudasai* 'two return **tickets** to Osaka please'. In Japanese it is necessary to use counters when specifying the number of objects being counted. The type of counter used depends on the type of object being counted. Here are three key categories:

For flat objects (tickets, postcards, letters):   *–mai*
For tubular objects (bottles, pens, flowers):   *–hon, –pon*
For 'lumps' of things:   *–ko*

kippu (o) san-mai kudasai   *please give me three tickets*
biiru (o) ni-hon kudasai   *two bottles of beer please*
akai bara no hana o juppon   *I bought ten red roses*
   kaimashita
chokorēto o ni-ko kudasai   *please give me two (of those) chocolates*

---

**RENSHŪ 1.2**

Here are three conversations at the ticket office where Tim bought his tickets to Osaka. Listen to them and then complete the table below. If the person reserves a seat, also give the time of the train.

|  | 1 | 2 | 3 |
|---|---|---|---|
| Single or return? | | | |
| How many tickets? | | | |
| Reserved/unreserved? | | | |
| How much? | | | |
| Platform number? | | | |
| Train departing at? | | | |

**BUNPŌ**    *Making comparisons*

Ōsaka ni wa 10.15 no hō ga hayaku        *the 10:15 gets to Osaka earlier*
    tsukimasu

The phrase . . . *no hō ga* . . . literally means 'the side of . . .'. It is used to convey comparison between two things or two ideas.

Tōshiba no konpyūtā to IBM no to        *Which are more expensive, Toshiba*
    dochira ga takai desu ka                *computers or IBM computers?*
IBM no konpyūtā no hō ga takai          *IBM computers are more expensive*
    desu                                          *(literally, the side of IBM computers*
                                                    *is more expensive)*

A fuller pattern to express comparison is: '*X' no hō ga 'Y' yori takai desu*, meaning '*X* is more expensive than *Y*'. If it is obvious (as in the above example) what the two things being contrasted are, the '*Y' yori* part can be left out. If it is necessary to make clear a comparison, the '*Y' yori* part should be used.

densha no hō ga basu yori hayaku        *the train arrives earlier than the bus*
    tsukimasu
Nihon wa Igirisu yori jinkō ga ōi        *is the population of Japan bigger (more*
    desu ka                                        *numerous) than Britain's?*

**RENSHŪ 1.3**

**a** Tim attended a presentation in Osaka which compared the size and age of the Osaka and Hiroshima *shisha* (branch offices) of Nihon Kōgyō. If you were making comments about the same statistics to a Japanese colleague, how would you make them? Use this pattern:

**Rei**   Ōsaka shisha no ho ga ōkii desu        *the Osaka office is bigger*

|                      | **Employees** | **When built** |
| -------------------- | ------------- | -------------- |
| **Ōsaka shisha**     | 26 000-nin    | 45 years ago   |
| **Hiroshima shisha** | 13 000-nin    | 20 years ago   |

1   Bigger (use *ōkii*)
2   Smaller (use *chiisai*)
3   Older (use *furui*)
4   Newer (use *atarashii*)

**b** Using the same pattern, comment on the following data:

1   *Nihon Kōkū* (Japan Airlines) 130 planes vs. *Zen Nikkū* (All Nippon Airways) 250 planes.
2   *Toyota Jidōsha* (Toyota Motor Corporation) founded 50 years ago vs. *Nissan Jidōsha* (Nissan Motor Corporation) founded 45 years ago.
3   *IBM no PC no māketto sheā* (share of PC market) 34 per cent vs. *Appuru* (Apple) 25 per cent.

🔊 **RENSHŪ 1.4**

Tim has lunch with Japan Industrial colleagues in Osaka. Listen to some of the business chat as well as some of the office gossip which Tim overhears. Then look at the options shown below and decide for yourself which are correct – such as who drank the most at the party last night! Tick the box corresponding to the answer given

| | | | | |
|---|---|---|---|---|
| 1 | Saturday | ☐ | Sunday | ☐ |
| 2 | April | ☐ | December | ☐ |
| 3 | 3.40 | ☐ | 4.05 | ☐ |
| 4 | Hayashi | ☐ | Katō | ☐ |
| 5 | Pari shisha | ☐ | Rondon shisha | ☐ |

**KAIWA NI** *Kesa wa isogashikatta kara, asa-gohan o tabete imasen*

**Jikan** Gozen, jūichiji-han
**Basho** Shinkansen no naka
**Jinbutsu** Timu-san to Ueda-buchō

🔊 Study these expressions. Then listen to them on cassette and repeat them in the pauses provided.

| | |
|---|---|
| kesa | *this morning* |
| isogashikatta | *was busy* |
| nanimo | *nothing* |
| nanika | *something* |
| tabetai desu | *I want to eat* |
| shanai hanbai no hito | *steward/stewardess (person selling things on board a train)* |
| makunouchi-bentō | *lunchbox consisting of small rice-balls* |
| chirashizushi | *'scattered' sushi* |
| nomitai desu | *I want to drink* |

Kaiwa ni o kiite kudasai:

TIMU: Kesa wa isogashikatta kara, asa-gohan o tabete imasen. Ueda-san wa?

UEDA: Watashi mo asa kara nanimo tabete imasen. Nanika tabetai desu ne. A, shanai-hanbai no hito ga kimashita.

TIMU: Watashi wa makunouchi-bentō ga tabetai desu. Sore kara, biiru mo nomitai desu ne.

UEDA: Sumimasen, makunouchu-bentō to chirashizushi o kudasai. Biiru mo ni-hon kudasai. Ikura desu ka.

HITO: Zenbu de ¥2400 (ni-sen yon-hyaku en) desu.

**BUNPŌ**

## *Saying when you haven't yet done something*

| | |
|---|---|
| asa-gohan o tabete imasen | *I haven't eaten breakfast yet* |

The form *–te imasen* means '(still) have not', i.e. a continuous state of not having done something:

| | |
|---|---|
| mada denwa o shite imasen | *I have not telephoned yet* |
| nani mo tabete imasen | *I have not eaten anything yet* |
| Tanaka-san no repōto o mada yonde imasen | *I have not read Tanaka's report yet* |

### RENSHŪ 2.1

Here is a selection of mini-conversations between staff at Japan Industrial about things they have done, are doing or haven't done yet. Listen to the conversations and decide what the state of play is for each. Mark the list below with an appropriate symbol from the choices shown:

○    the action has been completed
△    the action is going on at the moment
×    the action has not started yet

| **Rei** | mō kakimashita | *I've written it* | ○ |
|---|---|---|---|
| | ima kaite imasu | *I'm writing it now* | △ |
| | mada kaite imasen | *I haven't written it yet* | × |

1   Type up a report for a meeting.
2   Go to buy a coffee.
3   Telephone Mr Ueno.
4   Go to a new restaurant.
5   Meet the new trainee.

### RENSHŪ 2.2

a Maki Morita has popped out at lunchtime to buy a few things for herself and for the office. How would she have asked for the following items? Say how much they are each, and how much they are altogether. Remember to use the counting words (*–mai*, and *–hon*) if you can!

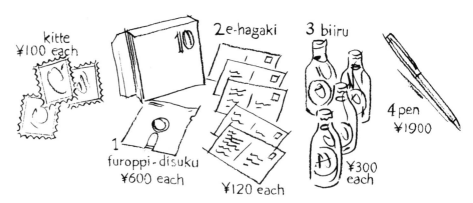

**Rei**  Hyaku-en kitte san-mai wa, san byaku-en desu

*100 yen stamps – three of them – are ¥300*

1   Furoppi-disku
2   E-hagaki

3   Biiru
4   Pen

**b** Now imagine *you* are asking a shopkeeper for these same items. How would you ask? **Use:** . . . *o kudasai* Give me . . . please.

**Rei**  Ten floppy disks please→*Furoppi-disku o jū-mai kudasai.*

1   Five picture postcards please.
2   Four bottles of beer please.
3   A pen please.

---

**BUNPŌ**

## The past tense of adjectives

*Isogashikatta desu* 'was busy' is an example of an adjective in the past tense (affirmative). It is derived from *isogashii* 'busy'.

### Formation
For –*i* adjectives, omit the –*i* and add –*katta*: takai→*takakatta* (*desu*) 'was expensive'. For –*na* adjectives, add *deshita*: genki→*genki deshita* 'was healthy'.

---

**RENSHŪ 2.3**

It's Monday morning again at Japan Industrial. Everyone is having a cup of tea or coffee in the rest area. There's a lot of joking going on about what went on over the weekend. Look at the pictures opposite and see whether you can recreate some of the conversations using the English prompts as starting points (hint: you'll need to use the past tense of adjectives).

### Rei
A:   Kyōnen no natsu doko ni ikimashita ka.
B:   Kagoshima ni ikimashita.
A:   Kagoshima wa dō deshita ka.
B:   Atsukatta desu.

rei — atsui (hot)    1 tanoshii (enjoyable)    oishii (delicious)    3 omoshiroi (interesting)    4 genki (fit, well)

1  Yesterday at a party. Enjoyable.
2  Last Saturday at an Italian restaurant to eat a (delicious, large) pizza.
3  On Sunday at the cinema. Interesting.
4  This morning to see Mr Komori who is in hospital. He seemed well.

**NARAIMASHŌ**  *The seasons*

haru *spring*    natsu *summer*    aki *autumn*    fuyu *winter*

**NARAIMASHŌ**  *Saying 'something'* (nanika) *and 'nothing'* (nanimo)

Try to familiarise yourself with other words that perform a similar job to *nanika* and *nanimo*:

dareka *someone*    daremo *no one*    dokoka *somewhere*    dokonimo *nowhere*

---

**RENSHŪ 2.4**

When Tim got back from his business trip, he realised that he had quite forgotten to buy any *omiyage* (souvenirs). This dawned on him when he had this short exchange with Maki Morita.

| | |
|---|---|
| MAKI: Nanika kaimashita ka. | *Did you buy anything?* |
| TIMU: Iie, nanimo kaimasen deshita. | *No, I did not buy anything.* |
| MAKI: Hontō-ni. | *Really?* |
| TIMU: Huh. A-a, sō ka. | *Huh? O-oh.* |

Now see whether you can complete the following dialogues.

1  **A:** Kinō dareka kimashita ka.
   **B:** Iie, .......... kimasen deshita.

2  **A:** Kyō nanika urimashita ka.
   **B:** Iie, .......... urimasen deshita.

3  **A:** Senshū dokoka ni ikimashita ka.
   **B:** Iie, .......... ikimasen deshita.

**BUNPŌ**   *Saying you want to or wish to do something*

To want to or wish to do something is expressed in Japanese by using the *–tai* form of the verb:

Hanbāgā o tabetai desu            *I'd love to eat a hamburger*
O-cha ga nomitai desu            *I'd like to drink some tea*

The choice about whether to use *o* or *ga* depends on the degree of desire on the part of the speaker: using *ga* normally indicates a higher degree of desire than *o*. Note that the *–tai* form is a very personal form and is therefore used almost exclusively in the first person.

**RENSHŪ 2.5**

Listen to the cassette. A group of executives from Japan Industrial are in the United States visiting a new green-field site. It's Sunday now, and they are just finishing off a day's sightseeing. The tour leader is telling them that they have some free time (*jiyū jikan*) before dinner back at their hotel. Find out where they are going and what they are going to do by listening in, matching the person with the place, and making a note of what they'll do once there.

1  Tanaka          **a** camera shop
2  Nakano          **b** post office
3  Mori             **c** café
4  Katō             **d** department store
5  Takeda           **e** bank

kissaten      *coffee shop*
o-kane        *money*
e-hagaki      *picture postcards*

**KAIWA SAN**   *Kono mae wa densha ni norimashita ga, hayakunakatta desu*

**Jikan**      Gogo ichiji-han goro
**Basho**      Shinkansen no eki kara Ōsaka Kagaku (*Osaka Chemicals*) made
**Jinbutsu**   Timu-san to Ueda-buchō

Study these expressions. Then listen to them on cassette and repeat them in the pauses provided.

| | |
|---|---|
| kono mae | *before now* |
| norimashita | *got on (a bus, train, plane)* |
| hayakunakatta | *was not fast, was not quick* |
| ano mon | *that gate* |
| massugu | *straight* |
| migi | *right (side)* |
| magatte kudasai | *please turn* |
| o-tsuri | *change* |
| ryōshūsho | *receipt* |

Kaiwa san o kiite kudasai:

TIMU:       Ōsaka Kagaku made nan de ikimasu ka.
UEDA:       Kyō wa takushii de ikimasu. Kono mae wa densha ni norimashita ga, hayakunakatta desu.
TIMU:       A sō desu ka. Wakarimashita.
UEDA:       Sumimasen. Ōsaka Kagaku made itte kudasai.
UNTENSHŪ:  Hai, wakarimashita.
UEDA:       A, ano mon o haitte, massugu itte, migi ni magatte kudasai. Hai, dōmo. Koko de ii desu.
UNTENSHŪ:  ¥3600 desu. ¥400 no o-tsuri desu.
UEDA:       Ryōshūsho onegai shimasu.
UNTENSHU:  Ryōshūsho desu ka. Hai, dōzo.

**NARAIMASHŌ**   Forming the negative past tense of adjectives

hayakunakatta desu                         *it wasn't quick*

*Hayakunakatta desu* is an example of an adjective in the past tense (negative). It is derived from the adjective *hayai* 'quick' or 'fast'.

**Formation**
For –*i* adjectives: *takai→takakatta→takakunakatta (desu)*
For –*na* adjectives: *genki desu→genki deshita→genki dewa arimasen deshita*

kyonen made uchi no kōhii wa          *up to last year, the coffee here (at our*
  oishikunakatta desu                        *company) was awful (i.e. not*
                                             *delicious)*

**RENSHŪ 3.1**

Tim and Ueda-san began their day at Osaka Kagaku by having a cup of coffee with one of Ueda-san's university chums, Iwamoto-san. Iwamoto-san has worked at the Osaka office for years and is Ueda-san's eyes and ears in the Osaka area. Tim listens patiently as Iwamoto chats on about changes at work and in the local area. See whether you can fill in what Iwamoto said. (Hint: You'll need to use the negative past tense of adjectives)

1   Kyonen no fuyu wa totemo .......... desu. Demo kotoshi wa totemo samui desu.

2   Kyonen made Furansu-go wa .......... desu. Demo ima wa totemo muzukashii desu.

3   Senshū, shigoto wa .......... desu. Demo, konshū wa totemo isogashii desu.

4   Kyonen made eki-mae no resutoran wa ........... Demo ima wa totemo yūmei desu.

### RENSHŪ 3.2

Iwamoto-san takes Ueda-san and Tim on a tour of the Osaka office, showing them recently purchased equipment and pointing out various reports and documents. Take a look at the pictures of the three men in the office and listen to the cassette. You'll hear Iwamoto-san talking to Ueda-san and Tim. Before attempting to answer the questions which follow, check that you understand the following words by studying the explanatory pictures **a**, **b** and **c**:

| **a** kore | *this (by me)* |
|---|---|
| kono pen | *this pen (by me)* |

| **b** sore | *that (next to you)* |
|---|---|
| sono pen | *that pen (next to you)* |

| **c** are | *that (over there, away from both of us)* |
|---|---|
| ano pen | *that pen (over there, away from both of us)* |

Iwamoto-san shows Ueda-san and Tim around the Osaka office

Iwamoto-san is doing the talking. Now answer these questions by circling the appropriate letter:

| | | |
|---|---|---|
| 1   Which fax machine was the more expensive? | A B | |
| 2   Which report was the better written and easier to understand? | A B | |
| 3   Which word processor was the newer and easier to use? | A B | |
| 4   Which documents does Iwamoto-san tell them to read? | A B C | |

**BUNPŌ**

## Connecting a series of actions using the –te form

The *–te* form of the verb can be used to connect a series of actions:

E o **mite**, renshū o shite kudasai
*look at the pictures and then do the exercises* (from *mimasu* 'to look at')

denwa bangō o mō ichido **shirabete**, denwa shite kudasai
*please look up the number again and then make the call* (from *shirabemasu* 'to look up')

dētā o **matomete**, repōto o kakimasu
*I'll collate the data and then write the report* (from *matomemasu* 'to gather together')

---

**RENSHŪ 3.3**

Imagine that you are going on a company visit to a client in Japan. Practise the following key directions as you would say them to a taxi driver (the *untenshu-san*).

massugu itte kudasai      migi ni magatte kudasai      hidari ni magatte kudasai

tsugi no shingō o migi ni magatte kudasai        tsugi no kōsaten o hidari ni magatte kudasai

shingō        *traffic light*
kōsaten       *crossroads, junction*

Remember that you can use the *–te* form of the verb to connect two actions which happen in sequence, e.g. go straight on *and then* turn right.

Kono mama massugu itte, tsugi no kōsaten o migi ni magatte kudasai

How would you give the following directions?

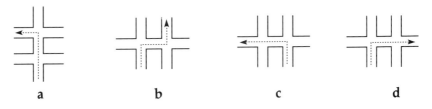

a          b          c          d

Now listen to the tape and check if your answers were correct.

## KAIWA YON  *Okuremashite, dōmo mōshiwake arimasen*

**Jikan**    Gogo san-ji goro
**Basho**    Nihon Kōgyō no shitauke no YMK no uketsuke de (*in the reception
             area of YMK, a Japan Industrial subcontractor*)
**Jinbutsu**  Ueda-san to Timu-san, uketsuke no hito to Nagata-san

 Study these expressions. Then listen to them on cassette and repeat them in the
pauses provided.

| | |
|---|---|
| (o-) yakusoku | *appointment* |
| betsu-no | *another* |
| o-kyaku-sama | *guest* |
| okuremasu | *be late* |
| mukō | *over there* |
| okuremashite | *on being late* |
| dōmo mōshiwake arimasen | *I'm very sorry* |
| o-hiru | *lunch* |
| o-tabe ni narimashita ka | *(honorific) have you eaten?* |
| zannen desu | *a pity, a shame* |
| go-annai shitakatta | *I wanted to show you, take you to* |
| kedo | *however* |
| shikata ga nai desu | *it cannot be helped* |
| tanoshimi ni shite imasu | *I look forward to . . .* |
| go-shōkai shimasu | *let me introduce . . .* |

 Kaiwa yon o kiite kudasai:

UEDA:         Nihon Kōgyō no Ueda desu. Nagata-buchō to ni-ji ni
              o-yakusoku o shite imasu.

UKETSUKE NO HITO: Shōshō o-machi kudasai. Mōshiwake arimasen. Nagata wa ima betsu no o-kyaku-sama to hanashi o shite imasu kara, juppun gurai okuremasu.

UEDA: Dewa mukō de matte imasu.

NAGATA: Ā, okuremashite, dōmo mōshiwake arimasen.

UEDA: A, Nagata-buchō. O-hisashiburi desu.

NAGATA: Mō o-hiru o o-tabe ni narimashita ka.

UEDA: Hai, mō tabemashita.

NAGATA: Sore wa zannen desu ne. Oishii sushiya ni go-annai shitakatta kedo, shikata ga nai desu ne.

UEDA: Dewa mata kono tsugi o tanoshimi ni shite imasu. Go-shōkai shimasu. Kochira wa Timu Gurosutā desu.

**BUNPŌ**

## Saying you didn't want to do something

Learn the affirmative and negative permutations of the –*tai* form.

| | | | |
|---|---|---|---|
| shitai | shitakunai | shitakatta | shitakunakatta |
| *I want to do* | *I don't want to do* | *I wanted to do* | *I didn't want to do* |
| tabetai | tabetakunai | tabetakatta | tabetakunakatta |
| *I want to eat* | *I don't want to eat* | *I wanted to eat* | *I didn't want to eat* |
| mitai | mitakunai | mitakatta | mitakunakatta |
| *I want to see* | *I don't want to see* | *I wanted to see* | *I didn't want to see* |

**RENSHŪ 4.1**

Back at the office in Tokyo, Tim is surprised to find Maki Morita looking despondent. To give you a clue as to why she is looking miserable, have a look at the pictures below. Then see whether you can work out the reasons for Maki's lack of cheer by completing the sentences which follow. You will need to use the past tense of the –*tai* form.

1  Kōhii o .......... kedo, o-kane ga arimasen deshita.

2  Sushi o .......... kedo, mise wa yasumi deshita.

3  Hon o .......... kedo, ii hon ga arimasen deshita.

4  Tomodachi ni .......... kedo, shigoto ga isogashikute, jikan ga arimasen deshita.

5  Eiga o .......... kedo, jikan ni okuremashita.

### RENSHŪ 4.2

Listen to the cassette to hear some people from Japan Industrial saying how they wanted or didn't want to do something. Make sure you are familiar with the following form of the verb before listening to the cassette.

tabetai       →    tabetakunai      →    tabetakunakatta
*want to eat*    →    *don't want to eat*    →    *didn't want to eat*

After listening to the conversations on cassette, choose the correct answer to the following questions, and supply the reasons as appropriate:

1   The person (wanted/didn't want) to go on business trip.
    Why? Because . . .

2   The person (wanted/didn't want) to go to the party.
    Why? Because . . .

3   The person (wanted/didn't want) to go to the director's house.
    Why? Because . . .

4   The person (wanted/didn't want) to drink beer.
    Why? Because . . .

**BUNPŌ**

## *Honorifics in Japanese*

mō o-hiru o o-tabe ni narimashita      *would you happen to have eaten already?*
   ka

*Tabe ni narimashita* is an honorific form of the verb *tabemasu* 'to eat'. Honorific verb forms are used if a speaker wishes to show respect to a person when speaking directly to them, or when talking about them to someone else. Using the stem of the verb plus *ni narimasu* 'to become', prefixed with the honorific *o–*, makes an honorific form; that is, a more polite version of the verb. *Tabemasu* goes to: *o-tabe ni narimasu*. This still means 'is eating', but is more polite than the *–masu* form. An English equivalent *feel* might be 'is partaking of . . .'
     With *–te kudasai* ('please' . . .) the more polite version is: *tabete kudasai* → *o-tabe ni natte kudasai* **or** *o-tabe kudasai*.
     Some verbs (formed from a noun plus a verb) just add *go* to the noun:

go-shōkai shimasu                       *let me introduce you to . . .*
go-annai shimasu                         *let me show you to . . .*
go-setsumei shimasu                   *allow me to explain to you . . .*
go-yōi shimasu                            *allow me to prepare . . . for you*

Other verbs like *denwa shimasu* make their polite forms in this way:

Morita-san ni o-denwa o nasaimashita     *would you happen to have telephoned Mr*
   ka                                       *Morita?*

In this case the polite form of *shimasu* 'to do' is *nasaimasu*.
     Sometimes a speaker may feel they have to speak using these polite forms – even if he or she does not respect the person they are talking about!

## RENSHŪ 4.3

Tim has started to come across some verbs which look vaguely related to ones he has already learned, but which feel somehow different, like: *o-tabe kudasai*, which he guesses has something to do with *tabemasu* 'to eat' and *tabete kudasai* 'please eat'.

Try changing these verbs into honorific forms, and then think of what the possible English equivalent might be:

1   Mō kōhii o nomimashita ka.

2   Purezento o kaimasu ka.

3   Kesa shimbun o yomimashita ka.

4   Sono nyūsu o kikimashita ka.

5   Itsu kaerimasu ka.

## RENSHŪ 4.4

Tim is beginning to learn that people in Japan expend quite a lot of energy on apologising. Sometimes the apology is legitimate, while at other times, it is used as an excuse. Listen to the cassette to find out why these people apologised or were apologised to. Put the number of the relevant picture next to their name:

a  Morita
b  Katō
c  Sumisu
d  Jon
e  Tanaka

## FUKUSHŪ

### FUKUSHŪ 1

Answer these questions about the four main *kaiwa* in this chapter.

1  9.50 no Shinkansen to 10.15 to dochira no hō ga hayaku Ōsaka ni tsukimasu ka.

2  Timu-san wa asa-gohan o tabemashita ka.

3  Shinkansen no naka de Ueda-san to Timu-san wa nani o kaimashita ka.

4  Ueda-san tachi wa eki kara Ōsaka Kagaku made nan de ikimashita ka. (–*tachi* is a suffix indicating plurals. Here meaning 'Ueda and the others with him'.)

5  Nagata-buchō wa dōshite juppun gurai okuremashita ka.

### FUKUSHŪ 2

Use the English prompts to make dialogues in Japanese.

**1  At the ticket office**
A:       *To Osaka, one return ticket please.*
CLERK: Jiyūseki desu ka.
A:       *Yes. How much is it?*
CLERK: 18 000-en desu.

**2  At the office**
A:  *I went to the party yesterday.*
B:  Pātii wa dō deshita ka.
A:  *It was enjoyable. I met Mr Suzuki.*

**3  In the taxi**
A:       *Go straight ahead, as it is, please.*
DRIVER: Hai, wakarimashita.
A:       *Please turn right at the next traffic light.*

### FUKUSHŪ 3

Choose the odd one out in each row.

| 1 | atsukatta | tabetakatta | samukatta | ōkikatta |
| 2 | nomitakunai | omoshirokunai | muzukashikunai | furukunai |
| 3 | hayaku | osoku | kyaku | nagaku |
| 4 | dokoka | tōka | yōka | yokka |
| 5 | massugu | hidari | yori | migi |

## FUKUSHŪ 4

These sentences each have an error which makes them rather strange. Can you spot the mistakes and correct them?

1  Kyō wa mada kōhii o nomimasen deshita kara, kōhii o nomitai desu.
2  Kinō wa shigoto ni ikitakunai deshita ga, ikimashita.
3  Kore pen wa takai deshita kedo, kaimashita. (*two mistakes*)
4  Shinkansen wa kuruma yori osoi desu.
5  Mōshiwake arimasen ga, ima nanika tabetakunai desu.

##  FUKUSHŪ 5

Tim went to the supermarket, where a barker was shouting out the day's bargains. Listen to find out how much the items were and how many he had to buy. Write your answers in the spaces below.

| | How many | How much |
|---|---|---|
| Biiru | | |
| Orenji jūsu | | |
| Biifu | | |
| Taoru | | |

## FUKUSHŪ 6

Listen to the dialogues and answer the following questions.

1  a  How much was a doughnut today?
   b  How much did a doughnut cost last week?
2  a  Can you get to the station earlier by taxi or by train?
   b  How long did it take by taxi to get to the station?
3  a  Why did the person apologise first?
   b  When was the lady's birthday?
4  a  Why did the man want to return home early?
   b  What did the lady offer him?

## FUKUSHŪ 7

How would you say the following in Japanese?

1  Two returns to Kyoto please.
2  This word processor was not expensive.
3  I haven't met the new company president yet.
4  I didn't go anywhere on Sunday.
5  Go straight ahead and then turn left please.
6  I'm terribly sorry to be late.
7  I wanted to play golf, but there was no time.
8  I'm sorry to telephone you late at night.
9  Have you read this report? (*said to a superior*)
10  I have an appointment with Mr Toda at 2.00 p.m.

### FUKUSHŪ 8

Rōrupurē

You are going to buy a train ticket to Yokohama. Good luck!

**You**                                                                                    **Clerk**

One single to Yokohama please.

Is it reserved or non-reserved?

Non-reserved please.

That will be ¥2 450 please.

Excuse me, what time will the next train be?

At 11.45.

Which platform will it go from?

Number 4.

Thank you.

# SAIGO NI

Before moving on to the next lesson, make sure you can:

| | |
|---|---|
| • buy a train ticket | *Ōsaka made ōfuku ni mai kudasai* |
| • buy some food | *o-bentō o kudasai* |
| • buy something to drink | *biiru o ippon kudasai* |
| • give directions to a taxi driver | *massugu itte kudasai* |
| • use some polite expressions | *o-tabe ni narimashita ka* |
| • say that you haven't done something yet | *mada denwa o shite imasen* |
| • apologise | *mōshiwake arimasen* |
| • make some comparisons | *Nihon wa Igirisu yori ōkii desu* |

# *Ganbatte kudasai*

## GOOD LUCK!

In this lesson you will learn how to:
- say whether you like or dislike something
- ask someone about their likes and dislikes
- make a decision
- say you are good (or bad) at something
- give some details about yourself and your family

**KAIWA ICHI** *Nani ni shimashō ka*

**Jikan** Gogo shichi-ji goro
**Basho** Resutoran
**Jinbutsu** Timu-san to Ueda-buchō to Morita-san

Study these expressions. Then listen to them on the cassette and repeat them in the pauses provided.

| | |
|---|---|
| A-setto ni shimasu | *I'll have the A-set (from a fixed menu in a restaurant)* |
| nomimono | *a drink* |
| nani ni shimashō ka | *what shall we have?* |
| wain ni shimashō | *lets have the wine* |
| enryo shinaide kudasai | *please do without hesitation (don't be shy . . .)* |

Kaiwa ichi o kiite kudasai:

UEDA:    Nani ni shimasu ka.
MORITA: Watashi wa A-setto ni shimasu.
UEDA:    Sutātā wa yasai-sūpu de, mein kōsu wa chikin de, dezatō wa aisukuriimu desu ne. Timu-san wa?
TIMU:    Watashi mo A-setto ni shimasu.
UEDA:    Nomimono wa nani ni shimashō ka. Wain to biiru to dochira ni shimashō kā.
MORITA: Itaria ryōri desu kara, wain no hō ga ii deshō.
UEDA:    Ja, wain ni shimashō. Sā, kyō wa enryo shinaide takusan tabete kudasai.

---

**BUNPŌ**    *Making a decision*

watashi wa kōhii ni shimasu          *I'll have a coffee*

The pattern . . . *ni shimasu* is used to convey a decision or choice. If you are inviting someone to do something ('let's . . .') use the *–mashō* form:

| | |
|---|---|
| wain ni shimashō ka | *shall we have wine?* |
| ikimashō! | *let's go!* |
| machimashō ka? | *shall we wait?* |

To summarise:

| | |
|---|---|
| ikimasu | *I'll/we'll go (simple statement of fact)* |
| ikimashō | *let's go (the speaker is positive about the idea)* |
| ikimashō ka | *shall we go? (the speaker is offering a suggestion)* |
| ikimasen ka | *would you like to go? (the speaker is asking the listener's preference)* |

## RENSHŪ 1.1

Staff at Japan Industrial are trying to make decisions about various things. Listen to the conversations on the cassette to find out what they are talking about and decide in which order the conversations come. Then write down their final decision.

**Topic of discussion**          **Their decision**

1 a post in a football club
2 where to go for their summer holiday
3 the fee for a party
4 the date of Mr Nakata's welcome party
5 a present for their boss

## RENSHŪ 1.2

The following pictures show situations in and around the Japan Industrial offices where people are offering suggestions to other people. Change the verbs provided, remembering to use the –*mashō* form of the verb ('let's...').

| | | |
|---|---|---|
| 1 | Mado o .......... ka. | akemasu (*to open*) |
| 2 | Hiru gohan o tabe ni .......... ka. | ikimasu |
| 3 | Tegami o .......... ka. | yomimasu |
| 4 | Watashi no kuruma de .......... ka. | kaerimasu |
| 5 | Doa o .......... ka. | shimemasu (*to shut*) |

## RENSHŪ 1.3

Tim and his colleagues are preparing for their departmental party. There are lots of things to be done, and Tim has offered to help with some of them. Follow the example dialogue below, substituting the phrases below for the parts in italics:

**Rei**

TIMU:      *Kaigi-shitsu o yoyaku shimashō* ka.
HAYASHI:  Hai, onegai shimasu. *Kaigi-shitsu o yoyaku shite* kudasai. *Doko no kaigi-shitsu ni shimashō* ka.
TIMU:      *San-gai no kaigi-shitsu* ni shimashō.

1   Sushi-ya ni denwa o shimasu
    Doko no sushi-ya
    Eki-mae no sushi-ya

2   Nomimono o kaimasu
    Donna nomimono
    Biiru to jūsu

3   Shōtaijō o kakimasu
    Nani iro
    Aka to shiro
    (iro *colour*      aka *red colour*      shiro *white colour*)

4   Dezāto o yōi shimasu
    Donna dezāto
    Chiizu to mikan

5   Kameraman o tanomimasu
    Dare
    Watanabe-san
    (tanomimasu *ask a favour*)

## RENSHŪ 1.4

Imagine you are making a date with someone. Put the following sentences in the correct order to make a short dialogue . (Hint: start with **5**.)

1   Rokuji wa dō desu ka
2   Hai, hima desu
3   Ueno eki wa kaisatsu-guchi wa dō desu ka
4   Ja, issho ni eiga o mi ni ikimashō ka
5   Ashita no ban, hima desu ka
6   Ii desu ne. Doko de aimashō ka
7   Hai, daijōbu desu. Ja, ashita no rokuji ni aimashō
8   Ja, Ueno eki de nanji ni aimashō ka

### KAIWA NI — *Mō hitotsu tabete mo ii desu ka*

**Jikan**     12-ji goro
**Basho**     Resutoran
**Jinbutsu**  Timu-san to Ueda-buchō

 Study these expressions. Then listen to them on cassette and repeat them in the pauses provided.

| | |
|---|---|
| hajimete | *for the first time* |
| kondo de | *this time* |
| ni-kai me | *the second time* |
| gakusei no toki | *when I was a student* |
| sono toki | *at that time* |
| dake | *only* |
| sanshūkan | *(for a period of) three weeks* |
| muri | *impossible* |
| hajimemashita | *started* |
| shumi | *hobby* |
| zehi | *I'd love to* |
| tabete mo ii desu ka | *may I eat?* |

**NARAIMASHŌ**  *More information on counting things*

It is sometimes possible to avoid using counters, that is *ichi-mai, ni-hon* etc., by using the following system:

ikutsu *how many?*

| | | | | |
|---|---|---|---|---|
| 1 hitotsu | 2 futatsu | 3 mittsu | 4 yottsu | 5 itsutsu |
| 6 muttsu | 7 nanatsu | 8 yattsu | 9 kokonotsu | 10 tō |

ringo o futatsu kudasai                    *please give me two apples*

As you can see, it is particularly handy for shopping. Note that this system only goes up to ten. For amounts over ten, use the ordinary numerals: *jū-ichi, jū-ni*, etc.

---

Kaiwa ni o kiite kudasai:

UEDA: Timu-san, Nihon wa hajimete desu ka.

TIMU: Iie. Kondo de ni-kai me desu. Daigakusei no toki ni kimashita.

UEDA: Dono gurai Nihon ni imashita ka.

TIMU: Sono toki wa ni-shūkan dake deshita. Hontō wa san-shūkan gurai itakatta kedo, muri deshita.

UEDA: Shumi wa nan desu ka.

TIMU: Karate desu. Go-nen mae hajimemashita. Ichido karate dōjō o mi ni ikitai desu.

UEDA: Sō desu ka. Kondo go-annai shimashō ka.

TIMU: Ee zehi. Kono Itaria sarada, oishii desu ne. Mō hitotsu tabete mo ii desu ka.

UEDA: Dōzo dōzo. Ja, watashi mo . . . Sumimasen, Itaria sarada o futatsu onegai shimasu.

**RENSHŪ 2.1**

During their lunchbreak, Tim, Maki, Ueda *buchō* and Watanabe-san were all in the same department store, but were buying different things.

a  The sentences below mention differing amounts of the items bought by the four people from Japan Industrial. How many of each item are mentioned and what is their total cost?

1 dōnatsu          2 ringo          3 wain gurasu          4 koin

1  Dōnatsu wa hitotsu rokujū en desu. Dōnatsu mittsu wa ikura desu ka.

2  Ringo wa hitotsu hyaku en desu. Ringo yottsu wa ikura desu ka.

3  Wain gurasu wa hitotsu ni-sen en desu. Gurasu muttsu wa ikura desu ka.

4  Furui koin wa hitotsu san-man en desu. Furui koin itsutsu wa ikura desu ka.

 **b** Now listen to the cassette to discover who actually bought what:

1  Tim:

2  Ueda buchō:

3  Maki:

4  Watanabe-san:

**BUNPŌ**

## Asking permission

To ask permission to do something, use the pattern:

'verb' (in the –*te* form) + *mo ii desu ka*

| | |
|---|---|
| kaette mo ii desu ka | *can I go home now?* |
| tabete mo ii desu ka | *can I eat (this)?* |
| kiite mo ii desu ka | *can I ask (you something)?* |

To give or to refuse permission, say:

| | |
|---|---|
| hai, dōzo | *yes, go ahead please* |
| hai, ii desu | *yes, that's fine* |
| iie, dame desu | *no, you may not* |

 **RENSHŪ 2.2**

Look at the pictures below, listen to the cassette, and find out whether Tim is allowed to do these things or not. Put a tick or a cross in the box in the corner of the picture:

**NARAIMASHŌ**    *Saying 'when'*

kodomo no toki                  *when I was a child*
gakusei no toki                 *when I was a student*
sanjūgo-sai no toki             *when I was thirty-five years old*

The pattern 'noun' + *no toki* expresses the idea 'when' as in 'at the time when . . .'. It is not exclusive to past events as shown in these examples:

shutchō no toki                 *when I'm on a business trip*
benkyō no toki                  *when I'm studying*

---

**RENSHŪ 2.3**

Can you answer these questions?

1  Kodomo no toki, nani ni naritakatta* desu ka.
2  Gakusei no toki, donna supōtsu o shimashita ka.
3  Gakusei no toki, doko ni ikitakatta desu ka.
4  Shutchō no toki, dare to ikimasu ka.
5  Tesuto no toki, yoku benkyō shimasu ka.

*from: . . . *ni narimasu* 'to become' e.g. *sensei ni narimasu* 'become a teacher'

**KAIWA SAN**    *Sukiyaki ga suki desu*

**Jikan**      Gogo 7.30 goro
**Basho**      Resutoran. Timu-san no kangei-kai
**Jinbutsu**   Timu-san to Ueda-san to kaigaikakubu no minasan

Study these expressions. Then listen to them on cassette and repeat them in the pauses provided.

| | |
|---|---|
| Timu-san no tame ni | *for Tim* |
| kanpai | *a toast (cheers!)* |
| suki (desu) | *like* |
| kirai (desu) | *dislike* |
| tsuyoi (desu) | *strong* |
| atama | *head* |
| itai (deshō) | *it is (it'll be) painful* |

 Kaiwa san o kiite kudasai:

UEDA: Mina-san, kanpai no yōi wa ii desu ka. Soredewa, Timu-san no tame ni kanpai.

TIMU: Mina-san, dōmo arigatō gozaimasu.

UEDA: Timu-san wa sukiyaki ga suki desu ka.

TIMU: Hai, daisuki desu.

UEDA: Nihon-ryōri no naka de kirai na mono ga arimasu ka.

TIMU: Ēto, nattō ga kirai desu. Ichido tomodachi no uchi de tabemasita ga, zenzen oishikunakatta desu.

UEDA: Nattō wa watashi mo amari suki dewa arimasen. Sā mō ippai biiru o dōzo.

TIMU: Hai, itadakimasu.

UEDA: Timu-san, o-sake ga tsuyoi desu ne. Biiru, mō ni-hon me desu yo.

TIMU: Ashita wa atama ga itai deshō ne.

**BUNPŌ**

## *Saying you like or dislike something*

To express like or dislike, follow this pattern:

| | |
|---|---|
| 'something' ga suki desu | *I like something* |
| 'something' ga kirai desu | *I don't like something* |
| tenisu ga suki desu | *I like tennis* |
| gorufu ga kirai desu | *I don't like golf* |

**RENSHŪ 3.1**

a What things do you like and dislike? Tick the responses most appropriate to you.

1 Watashi wa supōtsu ga suki/kirai desu.

2 Watashi wa ongaku ga suki/kirai desu.

3 Watashi wa supōtsu ga suki/kirai desu.

**b** If you add *–na* to *suki* or *kirai* you can use them in expressions like:

| | |
|---|---|
| suki-na tabemono | *a favourite food* |
| kirai-na tabemono | *food I don't like ('a disliked food')* |

Choose an appropriate word to complete the sentences below.

**1** Watashi no suki-na supōtsu wa .......... desu.

**2** Watashi no suki-na ongaku wa .......... desu.

**3** Watashi no suki-na eiga wa .......... desu.

If you want to ask someone else about their likes and dislikes, ask:

| | |
|---|---|
| suki-na tabemono wa nan desu ka | *what kind of food do you like?* |
| kirai-na nomimono wa nan desu ka | *what kind of drink do you like?* |

 **RENSHŪ 3.2**

Listen to Tim and Maki saying what they like and dislike and put a tick (like) or a cross (dislike) against the appropriate response.

| | |
|---|---|
| daisuki (desu) | *like very much* |
| daikirai (desu) | *greatly dislike* |
| amari suki dewa arimasen | *don't like very much* |

| Sports | Music | Films | Food | Drink |
|---|---|---|---|---|
| Rugby | Classical | Love stories | Italian | Beer |
| Cricket | Rock | Sci-fi | Japanese | Whisky |
| Tennis | Folk songs | Comedy | Chinese | Sake |
| | | | French | Wine |

**NARAIMASHŌ** *Some more practice describing people and things*

Learn this pattern: 'topic 1' wa 'topic 2' ga 'adjective' desu.

Now look at a picture of Maki and Tim. Maki has long hair:

Maki-san *(t1)* wa kami *(t2)* ga nagai *(adj)* desu. (Literally 'as for Maki, (her) hair is long'.)

Note the following:

| | |
|---|---|
| āno kaisha wa māketingu ga subarashii desu | *that company's marketing is wonderful (lit. 'as for that company, (its) marketing is wonderful')* |
| watashi wa me ga warui desu | *my eyes are bad (lit. 'as for me, the eyes are bad')* |
| Tanaka-san wa atama ga ii desu | *Tanaka's clever (lit. 'as for Tanaka, his head is good')* |

---

### RENSHŪ 3.3

Choose appropriate words from the three columns to make logical sentences.

| | | | |
|---|---|---|---|
| 1 | Ano resutoran wa | ryō | ga ōkii desu. |
| 2 | Burajiru wa | taipu | ga tsuyoi desu. |
| 3 | Sono kaisha wa | māketingu | ga hayai desu. |
| 4 | Tanaka-san wa | chiimuwāku | ga yowai desu. |
| 5 | Watashi no kaisha wa | sābisu | ga ii desu. |

### RENSHŪ 3.4

Ueda *buchō* and Hyashi *kachō* are discussing the relative merits of two companies, one called Mai Koara and the other Toppu Wan. Listen to the cassette and mark in the boxes which the better company is in each category. Which company do they eventually decide upon?

| | Mai Koara | Toppu Wan |
|---|---|---|
| good after-sales service | ☐ | ☐ |
| quick service | ☐ | ☐ |
| good product quality | ☐ | ☐ |
| strong marketing | ☐ | ☐ |
| cheap price | ☐ | ☐ |
| final choice | ☐ | ☐ |

hinshitsu *quality*    nedan *price*

## NARAIMASHŌ  *Explaining when you're ill*

The pattern: 'part of body' *ga itai desu*, is a useful one – as Watanabe-san found out.

| | |
|---|---|
| atama ga itai desu | *my head hurts (lit. my head is painful)* |

**RENSHŪ 3.5**

Last week Watanabe-san didn't feel well and was wondering whether he
would make it to Tim's welcome party. He went to the doctor to try to find out
what was wrong. Put yourself in Watanabe-san's shoes and tell the doctor
about how you feel. Look at the pictures and study the dialogue which follows:

DOCTOR:  Dō shimashita ka.
YOU:      ......... ga itai desu.
DOCTOR:  Itsu kara desu ka.
YOU:      Kinō kara desu.

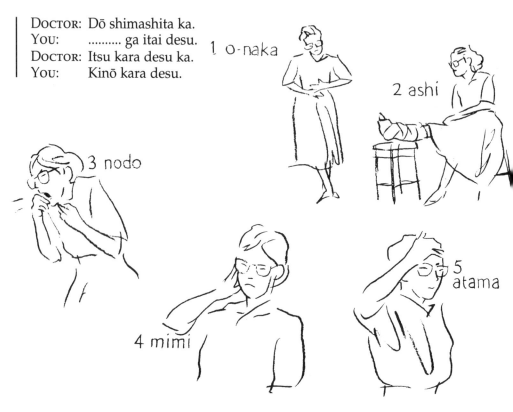

1 o-naka

2 ashi

3 nodo

4 mimi

5 atama

**KAIWA YON**  *O-hashi ga jōzu desu ne*

**Jikan**    Gogo 8-ji han goro
**Basho**    Resutoran
**Jinbutsu** Morita-san to Timu-san

Study these expressions. Then listen to them on the cassette and repeat them in the pauses provided.

| | |
|---|---|
| o-hashi | *chopsticks* |
| jōzu desu | *be good at* |
| tabe yasui | *easy to eat* |
| kazoku | *family* |
| (ni) tsutomete imasu | *work for/be employed by* |
| (ni) sunde imasu | *live in* |
| ni-kagetsu mae | *two months ago* |
| naratte imasu | *be learning* |
| heta desu | *be poor at* |
| ganbatte kudasai | *do your best* |

Kaiwa yon o kiite kudasai:

MORITA: Timu-san wa o-hashi ga jōzu desu ne.
TIMU: Hajime wa muzukashikatta desu yo. Ima wa fōku yori o-hashi no hō ga tabe yasui desu.
MORITA: Timu-san, go-kazoku wa.
TIMU: Watashi wa yo-nin kazoku desu. Chichi to haha to ane to watashi desu. Ane wa ginkō ni tsutomete imasu. Ni-kagetsu mae ni kekkon shite, ima Bāmingamu ni sunde imasu.
MORITA: Timu-san, Nihongo ga jōzu desu ne. Watashi wa mō san nen kan eigo o naratte imasu ga, mada heta desu. Hayaku jōzu ni naritai desu.
TIMU: Watashi mo o-tetsudai shimasu yo. Ganbatte kudasai.

**NARAIMASHŌ**  *Easy to do, difficult to do*

To say something is easy to do, take the stem of the verb and add *–yasui*:

| | | | | | |
|---|---|---|---|---|---|
| tabe masu | → | tabe– | → | tabeyasui | *easy to eat* |
| shimasu | → | shi– | → | shiyasui | *easy to do* |
| mimasu | → | mi– | → | miyasui | *easy to see* |

To say something is difficult to do, take the stem of the verb and add *–nikui*:

| | | | | | |
|---|---|---|---|---|---|
| tabe masu | → | tabe– | → | tabenikui | *difficult to eat* |
| nomimasu | → | nomi– | → | nominikui | *difficult to drink* |
| tsukaimasu | → | tsukai– | → | tsukainikui | *difficult to use* |

**RENSHŪ 4.1**

One of Japan Industrial's clients, a company which manufactures word processors, is planning a model change. Three designers are discussing the good and bad points of the old type. Listen to the cassette and draw how the new model might look after the improvements:

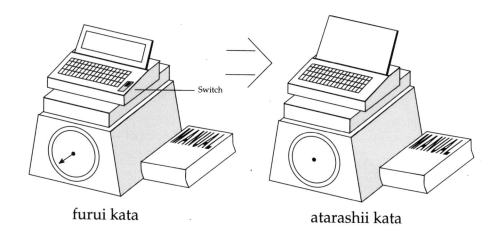

furui kata                    atarashii kata

kata *model*    karui *light*    omoi *heavy*

*Saying you're good or bad at something*

Study the following phrases:

| | |
|---|---|
| 'something' ga jōzu desu | *be good at/skilled at something* |
| 'something' ga heta desu | *be poor at something* |
| Furansugo ga jōzu desu | *he's good at French* |
| piano ga heta desu | *he's no good on the piano* |

 **RENSHŪ 4.2**

Listen to the cassette to hear details about three people who are seeking a job.
One wants secretarial work in a trading company, one wants to teach small
children English, and one wants to write articles for a publishing company.
You are an employer. Say who you think is the most suitable candidate for each
job, and give the reasons why:

**1**  Kimu-san            **2**  Katō-san            **3**  Kurāku-san

**NARAIMASHŌ**   *Giving details about yourself*

Some standard questions you are likely to be asked by Japanese colleagues are:

| | |
|---|---|
| doko ni sunde imasu ka | *where do you live?* |
| doko no kaisha ni tsutomete imasu ka | *what company are you employed by?* |
| kekkon shite imasu ka | *are you married?* |
| dokushin desu ka | *are you single?* |

Notice that in the first two questions, the verbs used are in the *–te* form, not the *–masu* form. This is because they describe your state. Answers to these questions might be:

| | |
|---|---|
| Rondon ni sunde imasu | *I live in London* |
| ICI ni tsutomete imasu | *I'm employed by ICI* |

If you want to say who your spouse is, say:

| | |
|---|---|
| Robin **to** kekkon shite imasu | *I am married to Robin* |

When you are out socialising you will almost certainly be asked about your family. So it's a good idea to practise talking about your family, and asking about others' families. Here is a list of some useful family terms; learn as many as you can.

| | terms for speaker's family<br>i.e. *my* family | terms for listener's family<br>i.e. *your* family |
|---|---|---|
| *family* | kazoku | go-kazoku |
| *parents* | ryōshin | go-ryōshin |
| *husband* | shujin | go-shujin |
| *wife* | kanai | okusan |
| *children* | kodomo | kodomo-san |
| *son* | musuko | musuko-san |
| *daughter* | musume | musume-san *or* o-jōsan |
| *older brother* | ani | o-niisan |
| *older sister* | ane | o-nēsan |
| *younger brother* | otōtō | otōto-san |
| *younger sister* | imōto | imōto-san |

And lastly: counting people. Learn the counters for people shown below:

| | | | |
|---|---|---|---|
| hitori | *one person* | nan-nin | *how many people?* |
| futari | *two people* | | |
| san-nin | *three people* | | |
| yonin | *four people* | | |
| etc. | | | |

How would you answer these questions about your family?

| | |
|---|---|
| go-kazoku wa nan-nin imasu ka | *how many people are there in your family?* |
| doko ni sunde imasu ka | *where do they live?* |
| doko ni tsutomete imasu ka | *where do they work?* |

## FUKUSHŪ

### FUKUSHŪ 1

Answer these questions about the four main *kaiwa* in this chapter.

1  Ueda-san tachi wa resutoran de nani o nomimashita ka.
2  Timu-san wa gakusei no toki dono gurai Nihon ni imashita ka.
3  Timu-san wa itsu karate o hajimemashita ka.
4  Timu-san no kirai na tabemono wa nan desu ka.
5  Timu-san no kazoku wa nan nin desu ka.
6  Timu-san no o-nēsan wa doko ni tsutomete imasu ka.

### FUKUSHŪ 2

Complete the dialogues in Japanese using the English prompts.

1  At a restaurant
A:  Nani ni shimasu ka.
B:  *I ate curry and rice yesterday, so I'll have spaghetti today.*
A:  Nomimono wa nani ni shimasu ka.
B:  *I'll have juice.*

2  At the office
A:  *May I use the large meeting room?*
B:  Ni-ji kara kaigi ga arimasu kara, chotto muzukashii desu ne . . .
A:  *May I use it tomorrow?*
B:  Hai, ashita wa ii desu yo.

3  At the office
A:  *It's cold isn't it? Shall I shut the window?*
B:  Hai, onegai shimasu.
A:  *It's still cold. May I switch on the heater?*
B:  Dōzo, dōzo, enryo shinaide kudasai.

4  At a party
A:  Go-ryōshin wa doko ni sunde imasu ka.
B:  *They live in Canberra.*
A:  Go-ryōshin wa Nihon-ryōri o o-tabe ni narimasu ka.
B:  *Yes, they like Japanese food.*

### FUKUSHŪ 3

Listen to the following dialogues and then answer the questions.

1  a  What is the matter with the lady?
   b  What is she going to do?
2  a  What did the lady buy?
   b  Which size did she decide on?

3   **a** What are they going to do on Sunday?
    **b** How does the lady get to her friend's house?
    **c** Will the lady buy any wine?

4   **a** What time do they go to the hospital?
    **b** Do you think they bought chocolates for Mr Tanaka?

## FUKUSHŪ 4

Try to fill in as much of the form, below, as you can.

---

# *Anketo*

1    O-namae wa?  – – – – – – – – – – – – – – – – – – – –

2    O-kuni wa?  – – – – – – – – – – – – – – – – – – – –

3    O-Shigoto wa?  – – – – – – – – – – – – – – – – –

4    O-tanjōbi wa itsu desu ka?  – – – – – – – – – –

5    Shumi wa nan desu ka?  – – – – – – – – – – – –

6    Kozoku wa nan nin imasu ka?  – – – – – – – –

7    Kazoku wa doko ni sunde imasu ka?  – – – – –

8    Doko de Nihongo o benkyō shimashita ka?  – – – – –

9    Dare to Nihongo o benkyō shimashita ka?  – – – – –

10   Itsu Nihon ni ikimasu ka?  – – – – – – – – – –

---

## FUKUSHŪ 5

How would you say the following in Japanese?

1  Please don't hesitate (help yourself).
2  Shall I shut the door?
3  May I open the window?
4  I bought three doughnuts.
5  I started judo when I was a child.
6  I have lived in Yokohama for five months.
7  When I was a student I studied Japanese.
8  I like tennis but I don't like golf.
9  Mr Katō is good at English.
10  This computer is easy to use.

### FUKUSHŪ 6

Rōropurē

You are walking along to your company canteen when you meet a Japanese colleague on the way.

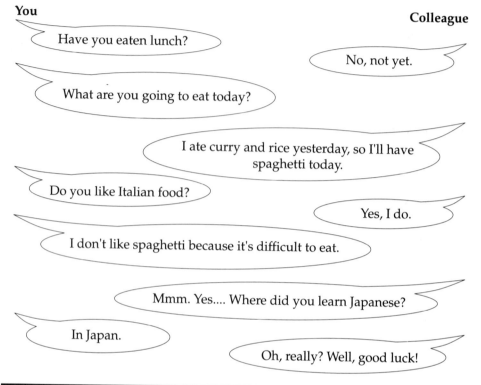

**You**                                                                    **Colleague**

Have you eaten lunch?

No, not yet.

What are you going to eat today?

I ate curry and rice yesterday, so I'll have spaghetti today.

Do you like Italian food?

Yes, I do.

I don't like spaghetti because it's difficult to eat.

Mmm. Yes.... Where did you learn Japanese?

In Japan.

Oh, really? Well, good luck!

# SAIGO NI

Before leaving this lesson, make sure you can:

| | |
|---|---|
| • say what you like | *tenisu ga suki desu* |
| • say what you don't like | *gorufu ga kirai desu* |
| • make a decision | *A-setto ni shimasu* |
| • make polite suggestions | *wain ni shimashō ka* |
| • refer to events in the past | *daigakusei no toki* |
| • ask permission to do something | *tabete mo ii desu ka* |
| • count using the *hitotsu, futatsu* system | |
| • make important small talk about your family and friends | *yon-nin kazoku desu* |

Good luck in the future with your Japanese! *Ganbatte kudasai!*

# GLOSSARY

aimasu    to meet with (usually takes ni)
Airurando    Ireland
akai    red
akarui    bright, cheerful
akemasu    to open
aki    autumn
amari . . . masen    not very (with negative)
Amerika    America
anaunsā    announcer
ane    older sister (speaker's)
ani    older brother (speaker's)
annai    guide, invite
aoi    blue
apāto    apartment, flat
apointo    an appointment
are    that one (over there)
arigatō gozaimasu    thank you very much
arimasen    does not exist, there is none
arimasu    to exist, be, (usu. with inanimate things)
aruite    by walking
asa    morning
asa-gohan    breakfast
ashi    leg, foot
ashita    tomorrow
asoko    over there away from both of us
atama    head
atarashii    new
atarashikunai    not new
atatakai    warm
ato    after
ato de    afterwards
atsui    hot

bāgen    bargain
ban    the evening
banana    banana
bangō    number
ban-gohan    evening meal, dinner
bara    a rose flower
basho    place, spot, location
basu    bus, bath
bengoshi    lawyer, solicitor
benkyō (shimasu)    (to) study
benri-na    convenient
bentō    lunch box
betsu no    another
biifu    beef
biiru    beer
bisuketto    biscuit
botan    a button
bu    department
buchō    general manager
bunpō    grammar

chichi    father (speaker's)
chigaimasu    it's different, wrong, no
chiimuwāku    team work

chiisai    small
chikai    near
chikaku    nearby
chikatetsu    the Underground, subway
chirashi zushi    a type of sushi
chizu    map
chō    an American trillion
chōdo    exactly, just right
chokorēto    chocolate
chotto. . .    rather. . ./a little
chū    suffix meaning while, during, in the middle of

daigaku    university, college
daigakusei    university/college student
daiji-na    important
daijōbu    all right, surely
daijōbu (desu)    fine, no problem
dake    only
dame desu    is not allowed, don't!
dare    who?
dareka    someone
daremo    nobody (with negative)
dare no    whose?
de    particle showing where an action happened/by means of
demo    however, but
denki    electric(ity)
densha    train
denwa    a telephone
denwa-bangō    telephone number
denwa-chū    on the telephone
depāto    department store
deshita    was
dewa mata    (I'll call/see you) again
dewa arimasen    is/am/are not
dezainā    designer
dezainbu    design department
dezāto    dessert
doa    door
dochira no hō ga    which one?
Doitsu    Germany
doko    where
dokoka    somewhere
dokushin    single, not married
donata    who (polite)
dōnatsu    doughnuts
donna    what kind of?
dore    which one?
doyōbi    Saturday
dōzo yoroshiku onegai shimasu    pleased to meet you

e    picture
e-hagaki    picture postcard
eiga    a cinema film, movie
eigo    English language
eigyōbu    marketing department
eki    station
en    Japanese Yen (¥)

enjinia    engineer
enryo    reserve
enryo shinaide kudasai    don't hesitate, help yourself
erebētā    elevator, a life

fairu    a file, box file
fakkusu    facsimile, fax
ferii    ferry
fuirumu    camera film
fukushū    review, revision
fune    boat
Furansu    France
Furansujin    a French national
furoppi    floppy disk
furui    old (not for people)
futari    two people
futatsu    two items
fuyu    winter

gaishutsu    being out of the office or home
gaishutsu-chū    in the middle of going out
gakkō    school
gakusei    student
ganbatte kudasai    do your best
genki    well, healthy, fit
getsuyōbi    Monday
ginkō    bank
go    five
gofun    five minutes
gogatsu    May
gogo    afternoon, p.m.
go-kazoku    family (listener's)
goro    about (used for a point in time)
gorufu    golf
go-ryōshin    both parents (listener's)
go-shujin    husband (listener's)
gozen    morning, a.m.
gurai    about
gurasu    drinking glass

hachi    eight
hachifun    eight minutes
hachigatsu    August
hagaki    postcard
haha    mother (speaker's)
hai    yes
hairimasu    to enter
hai sō desu    yes, that's right
hajimemashita    (it's) started
hajimemashite    how do you do (first meeting)
hajimete    for the first time
hako    a box
hambaibu    sales department
han    a half, (e.g. kuji-han, 9.30)
hana    flowers, nose
hanami    flower-viewing
hanashimasu    to speak, talk
hanbaibu    sales department

hanko    *Chinese seal, chop mark, signet*
hansamu na    *handsome*
happun    *eight minutes*
haru    *spring season*
hashi    *chopsticks*
hayai    *quick, early, rapid*
hayaku    *quickly*
hayakunakatta    *was not quick*
heta (desu)    *be poor at*
heya    *a room*
hidari    *the left*
hiitā    *heater*
hikōki    *plane*
hima    *free (time)*
hinshitsu    *quality*
hiroi    *spacious, wide*
hirokunai    *not spacious, cramped*
hiru    *midday, noon, day*
hiru-gohan    *lunch*
hisashiburi    *a long time*
hisho    *secretary*
hito    *person*
hitori    *one person*
hitori de    *by oneself, alone*
hitotsu    *one item*
hōmu    *station platform*
hon    *book*
hon    *a counter for tubular things*
honsha    *head office*
hontō    *really*
horidē    *a holiday*
hoteru    *hotel*
hyaku    *a hundred*

ichi    *one*
ichi-do    *once, one time*
ichigatsu    *January*
ichi-ji    *one o'clock*
ichiji-kan    *a period of one hour*
Igirisu    *Britain*
Igirisujin    *a British national*
ii    *good*
iie    *no*
iimasu    *to say*
ikaga    *how about . . . ? (polite)*
ikimashita    *went*
ikimasu    *to go*
ikkagetsu (kan)    *for one month*
ikura    *how much?*
ima    *now*
ima kara    *(from) now*
imasen    *not here, not available*
imasu    *to exist, be (usu. with animate things)*
imōto    *younger sister (speaker's)*
imōto-san    *younger sister (listener's)*
ippai    *one cupful*
ippai    *feel full*
ippun    *one minute*
isogashii    *busy*
isogashikatta    *was busy*
isogashikunai    *not busy*
issho ni    *together with someone*
isu    *chair*
itadakimasu    *I'll/we'll eat (polite)*
itai (desu)    *painful*
Itaria    *Italy*
itsu    *when?*

itsumo    *always*
itsutsu    *five items*
itte kudasai    *please say*

jidōsha    *car, automobile*
jikan    *time*
jimu-shitsu    *office room*
jinjibu    *personnel department*
jinkō    *population*
jippun    *ten minutes*
jiten    *dictionary*
jitensha    *bicycle*
jiyū-jikan    *free time*
jiyūseki    *non-reserved seat*
jōzu-na/ni    *well, skilled*
jū    *ten*
jūgatsu    *October*
jūichigatsu    *November*
jūnigatsu    *December*
juppun    *ten minutes*

ka    *sentence final particle indicating a question*
kaban    *briefcase, bag*
kachō    *manager*
kaerimashita    *went back, returned*
kaerimasu    *to return, go back*
kagaku    *chemicals, chemistry*
kagetsu    *counter for period of months*
kaigai    *overseas*
kaigi    *a meeting, conference*
kaigi-chū    *in a meeting*
kaigi-shitsu    *conference room*
kaihi    *membership fee*
kaimasu    *to buy*
kaimono    *shopping*
kaisatsu-guchi    *ticket gate*
kaisha    *the company*
kaisha no hito    *colleague*
kaiwa    *conversation*
kakarichō    *assistant manager*
kakarimasu    *(it) takes/costs*
kakimasu    *to write*
kamera    *camera*
kampai    *a toast, cheers!*
kamukōdā    *video camera*
kan    *suffix added to times to show duration of time*
Kanada    *Canada*
kanai    *wife (speaker's)*
kane    *money*
kangei-kai    *welcome party*
kanrinin    *caretaker*
kara    *from, after, because*
kare    *he*
karui    *light, not heavy*
kata    *shape, style, model*
katamichi    *one way (ticket)*
kawa    *river*
kawaii    *cute*
Kayōbi    *Tuesday*
kazoku    *family*
kedo    *but*
keiribu    *accounts department*
kekkō desu    *it's fine, I'm fine, I'll take it*
kekkon shite imasu    *to be married*
kekkyoku    *in the end, in the long run*
kenshūsei    *trainee, internee*

kesa    *this morning*
kibishii    *strict*
kikakubu    *planning department*
kikimasu    *to hear*
kimasu    *to come*
kinō    *yesterday*
kinyōbi    *Friday*
kippu    *fare ticket*
kirai (desu)    *dislike*
kirei ni/na    *beautiful/clean*
kissaten    *coffee shop*
kitte    *postage stamp*
ko    *a counter for spherical/lumpy things*
kō-cha    *tea*
kōchi    *coach, instructor*
kochira    *this is, in this direction*
kodomo    *children*
kōgyō    *industry*
kōhii    *coffee*
koin    *coin*
koko    *here*
kokonotsu    *nine items*
kondo de    *this time*
kongetsu    *this month*
kono mae    *before now*
kono mama    *as it is*
konpyūtā    *computer*
konsāto    *a concert*
konshū    *this week*
kopii-shitsu    *photocopy room*
koppu    *cup*
kore    *this one*
kōsaten    *crossroads, intersection*
kōsu    *course*
kugatsu    *September*
kuni    *country*
kurabu    *club*
kurasshiku    *classical (music)*
kurasu    *class*
kuroi    *black*
kuruma    *car*
kyaku    *guest*
kyaputen    *captain (of team)*
kyō    *today*
kyonen    *this year*
kyū    *nine*
kyūfun    *nine minutes*
kyūkei-shitsu    *rest room*
kyū-na    *sudden, unexpected*

machi    *town*
machimasu    *to wait*
mada desu    *not yet*
made    *until*
mado    *window*
mae    *in front of, before, opposite*
magarimasu    *to turn*
magatte kudasai    *please turn*
mai    *a prefix meaning 'every'*
mai    *a counter for flat things*
mainichi    *everyday*
maishū    *every week*
man    *a unit of 10000*
massugu    *straight ahead*
matomemasu    *to gather together, collate*
matte kudasai    *please wait*
me    *eye*
-me    *a suffix denoting*

*time/number/frequency*

mein kōsu   *main course of meal*
meishi   *business card*
messēji   *message*
migi   *the right*
miitingu   *a meeting*
mikan   *Japanese orange, satsuma*
mimasu   *to see*
mimi   *ear*
miruku   *milk*
mise   *shop*
misete kudasai   *please show me*
mittsu   *three items*
mō   *already*
mō ichido   *once more*
mokuyōbi   *Thursday*
mon   *gate*
mono   *thing*
moshi moshi   *hello, are you there?*
mōshiwake arimasen   *I'm very sorry*
motto   *more*
mugi-cha   *barley tea*
mukai-gawa   *opposite side*
mukō   *the other side, over there*
muri   *impossible*
mushiatsui   *stickily humid*
musuko   *son (speaker's)*
musuko-san   *son (listener's)*
musume   *daughter (speaker's)*
musume-san   *daughter (listener's)*
muttsu   *six items*
muzukashii   *difficult*

nagai   *long*
naka   *inside, middle*
namae   *name*
nan   *what? (same as* nani*)*
nana   *seven*
nanafun   *seven minutes*
nanatsu   *seven items*
nan-ban   *what number?*
nan-de   *by what means? (of transport)*
nandemo   *anything*
nani   *what?*
nanika   *something*
nanimo   *nothing (with negative)*
nan-ji   *what time?*
nan-nichi   *which day?*
nan-nin   *how many people?*
naraimasu   *to learn*
narimasu   *to become*
Narita kūkō   *Narita International
    Airport*
nasaimasu   *(honorific) to do*
natsu   *summer*
nattō   *fermented soybeans*
nedan   *cost, price*
ni   *a particle indicating a time or a place*
ni   *two*
ni arimasu   *located at, in . . .*
nichi   *day (in dates)*
nichiyōbi   *Sunday*
nifun   *two minutes*
nigatsu   *February*
Nihon   *Japan*
Nihoncha   *Japanese green tea*
Nihongo   *Japanese language*
Nihonjin   *a Japanese national*

nikagetsu (kan)   *for two months*
ni-kai me   *the second time*
nikui   *difficult to do*
no   *a particle showing possession*
nodo   *throat*
no toki   *when, at the time of*
nomimasu   *to drink*
nomimono   *a drink*
norimasu   *to board, ride on (a train etc)*
no hō ga   *in the direction of*
Nyū Jiirando   *New Zealand*
nyūsu   *news*

oboemashō   *let's remember!*
o-cha   *tea*
ofisu   *office*
ōfuku   *return ticket*
o-genki desu ka   *how are you*
ohayō   *good morning!*
ōi   *many*
oishii   *delicious*
o-jōsan   *daughter (listener's)*
o-kane   *money*
o-kāsan   *mother (listener's)*
ōkii   *big*
oku   *a hundred million*
okuremasu   *to be late*
okurimasu   *to send*
okusan   *wife (listener's)*
OL   *Office Lady*
o-machi kudasai   *please wait (polite)*
o-matase shimashita,   *I've kept you
    waiting*
o-miyage   *souvenir*
omoi   *heavy*
omoshiroi   *interesting*
omoshirokunai   *uninteresting*
o-naka   *stomach, abdominal area*
o-nēsan   *older sister (listener's)*
ongaku   *music*
o-niisan   *older brother (listener's)*
onna no hito   *a woman*
orenji   *orange*
osoi   *late, slow*
Ōsutoraria   *Australia*
o-taku   *someone else's house, residence*
o-tetsudai   *help*
oto   *a sound*
otoko no hito   *a man*
o-tōsan   *father (listener's)*
otōto   *younger brother (speaker's)*
otōto-san   *younger brother (listener's)*
otsukaresama   *well done! (lit. you are
    tired)*
o-tsuri   *change from money*
owarimasu   *to finish*

pātii   *a party*
pen   *pen*
piano   *piano*
piza   *pizza*
purattohōmu   *platform (station)*
purezentēshon   *a presentation*
purezento   *at present, gift*

ragubii   *rugby*
raigetsu   *next month*
raishū   *next week*

rajio   *radio*
ranchi   *lunch*
renshū   *practice*
repōto   *a report*
ressun   *lesson*
resutoran   *restaurant*
ringo   *apple*
robii   *lobby*
rokkā   *document cabinet, locker*
roku   *six*
rokugatsu   *June*
romanchikku   *romantic*
roppun   *six minutes*
ryō   *dormitory, quantity*
ryokō   *a trip, journey, travel*
ryōri   *cooking, cuisine*
ryōshin   *both parents*
ryōshūsho   *receipt*

sā . . .   *well . . .*
sābisu   *service*
sai   *suffix for age (years)*
saigo ni   *and finally*
saikuringu   *cycling*
saizu   *size*
sakkā   *soccer, football*
samui   *cold*
san   *three*
sandoitchi   *sandwiches*
sangatsu   *March*
sankagetsu (kan)   *for three months*
san-nin   *three people*
sanpun   *three minutes*
sarada   *salad*
saraishū   *week after next*
sen   *a thousand*
sengetsu   *next month*
sensei   *teacher*
senshū   *last week*
sērusuman   *salesman*
shachō   *company president*
shachō-shitsu   *company president's
    room*
shanai hanbai   *person selling food on
    board a train*
shashin   *photograph*
shi   *four*
shichi   *seven*
shichigatsu   *July*
shichi-ji   *seven o'clock*
shigatsu   *April*
shigoto   *one's work*
shikata ga arimasen   *it can't be helped*
shimasu   *to do*
shimbun   *newspaper*
shimemasu   *to close*
shingō   *traffic light*
shinkansen   *bullet train*
shinsetsu-na   *kind, helpful*
shirabemasu   *to investigate, look up*
shirimasu   *to know (a fact)*
shiroi   *white*
shiryō   *document*
shiryō-shitsu   *document room*
shisha   *branch office*
shita   *under*
shitauke   *a subcontractor*
shiteiseki   *reserved seat*

shizuka-na/ni    quiet
shōhin kaihatsubu    product development department
shōkai shimasu    to introduce
shokudō    restaurant, dining room
shokuji-chū    dining, at lunch
shōshō    a moment, a bit
shōtaijō    invitation card
shujin    husband (speaker's)
shumi    hobby
shutchō    business trip
shutchō-chū    on a business trip
soba    beside
soko    over there near you
sōmubu    general affairs department
sono toki    at that time
sore    that one (near you)
sorede    so, therefore, and
soredewa    in that case, then
sore kara    after that, and then
soshite    and
sugoi    amazing!
sugu    immediately
suiyōbi    Wednesday
sukejūru    schedule, itinerary
suki (desu)    like
sukiyaki    a Japanese beef dish
sukoshi    a few, slightly
Sukottorando    Scotland
sumimasen    I'm sorry; excuse me
sumimasu    to live in, reside
sūpā    supermarket
Supein    Spain
supōtsu sentā    sports centre
sūpu    soup
suraido    a slide
sushiya    sushi shop
suwarimasu    to sit
suzushii    pleasantly cool

tabemasu    to eat
tabemono    food, things to eat
tabetai    want to eat
tabe-yasui    easy to eat
taihen    awful, tough, very, extremely
taipu    type
takai    expensive, tall
takakunai    inexpensive
takusan    lots, many
takushii    taxi
tanjōbi    birthday
tanomimasu    to ask a favour
tanoshii    enjoyable
tanoshimi ni shite imasu    I'm looking forward to . . .
tēburu    table
tegami    a letter
-te mo ii desu ka    may I . . . ?
tenisu    tennis
tenki    weather
tēpu    a tape
terebi    television
tesuto    a test
tō    ten items
tō    ten
tokidoki    sometimes
tokoro    place
tomodachi    friend

tonari no    next to
torēningu    training
torimasu    to take (a photograph)
totemo    very
tsugi    the next
tsukaremshita    was tired
tsukemasu    to switch on, attach
tsukimasu    to arrive
tsukue    desk
tsumaranai mono    an insignificant thing
tsutaemasu    to communicate, tell
tsutaete kudasai    please tell
tsutomemasu    to be employed
tsuyoi    strong

uchi    home, house
ue    on top of, over
uisukii    whisky
uketsuke    reception area
umi    sea
urayamashii    enviable
urimasu    to sell
ushiro    behind
uta    song
utaimasu    to sing

wa    a particle marking the topic
wain    wine
wakarimashita    (I) understand
wakarimasu    to understand
wāpuro    Japanese typewriter
warui    bad
watashi    I, me
watashi no    my
watashitachi    we

yakitori    grilled chicken
yakusoku    appointment, promise
yama    mountain
yasai-sūpu    vegetable soup
yasashii    easy, kindly
yasui    cheap
yasumi    rest, holiday, day off
yattsu    eight items
yōi    preparations
yoko    side
yōkoso    welcome
yoku    often, well
yomimasu    to hear
yon    four
yonpun    four minutes
yori    a comparative meaning 'than'
yoru    night
yotei    schedule, plan
yottsu    four items
yūbinkyoku    post office
yubiwa    ring for finger
yukkuri    slowly
yūmei-na    famous

zannen desu    It's a pity, regrettable
zehi    absolutely, I'd love to
zenbu    all, in all
zenzen    never, not at all (with negative)